Reflections of a Love Supreme

Motown Through The Eyes of Fans

TOM INGRASSIA

Reflections of a Love Supreme
Motown Through the Eyes of Fans
Tom Ingrassia

Print Edition ISBN: 978-1-942545-29-3
eBook Edition ISBN: 978-1-942545-32-3

Library of Congress Control Number: 2015954835

© 2015 Tom Ingrassia
All rights reserved.

No part of this book may be reproduced or transmitted in any form or by any means without the written permission of the publisher, except in the case of brief quotations used in book reviews and articles.

Book Design by Nancy Cleary.

Front Cover Photo Credits:
1966 Official Supremes Fan Club Card (Courtesy of the author.)
Diana Ross and The Supremes arriving in London in January, 1968
(Courtesy of Jim Saphin.)

Back Cover Photo Credit:
Tom Ingrassia photo by Erb Photography.

MotivAct Publishing
An Imprint of Wyatt-MacKenzie

Dedication

I will never forget the summer of 1964—that is when I first fell in love with the music of Motown. From that point on, I could literally trace my life through that music—Motown provided the soundtrack to my life—just as it did for so many others in the '60s. Everything I do in life today—all the success I have achieved—started that summer, when I first heard The Supremes' "Where Did Our Love Go?" on my little transistor radio. This book is dedicated to all the great Motown artists who have provided over fifty years of happy listening and inspiration—especially Diana, Mary and Flo—the legendary Supremes. In particular, this book is dedicated to Mary Wilson—my mentor and teacher. You opened doors for me, for which I will always be grateful. It also is dedicated to my wife, Barbara, without whose support and love I would never have realized my dreams.

Table of Contents

The Music That Inspired A Generation... And Changed The World	13
The Many Faces of Motown	31
Motown and Detroit	63
The Supreme Dream	83
Motown On Stage and Around The World	111
Motown Is Forever	137
Epilogue: Reflections	173
Select Bibliography	177
Select Videography	179

Acknowledgments

There are so many people responsible for this book—this is a collection of photos taken by fans and from their private collections. Most of them have never been published before. Thank you to the following people who so generously shared their photos: Cindy Birdsong, Randall Wilson (author of *Forever Faithful: Florence Ballard & The Supremes*), Brad Adams, Linda DiStefano, Marie and Dan Leighton, Jim Saphin (from England), Ulf Wahlberg (from Sweden), Rusty Maghanoy, the late Jonathan Ptak, photojournalist Alex Atwell, Peter Benjaminson (author of *The Lost Supreme: The Life of Dreamgirl Florence Ballard* and *Mary Wells: The Tumultuous Life of Motown's First Superstar*), Dennis Lima, Robert Dana, and John Burke, Jr. Special thanks also to The Detroit News, for its contributions. I also have to give a shout-out to Troy Tyree, executive director of WCUW 91.3 FM, in Worcester, MA, who allows me the great privilege of hosting "The Jukebox of Motown" every Tuesday morning on the station. As a kid in the 1960s, I went to sleep every night with that little transistor radio tucked under my pillow, dreaming that one day I would be just like "Cousin" Brucie Morrow, Herb Oscar Anderson, Chuck Leonard and Dan Ingram—the WABC radio DJs I idolized. It took me 50 years—but, Troy, you made that dream come true!

Every effort has been made to identify and properly credit the owners of the photographs used in this book. In some cases, photographs taken by fans were not originally identified, and through the years information about their source has been lost.

Introduction

EVERY DECADE HAS its musical phenomenon. The 1960s had Motown—and Motown became the music that inspired a generation with artists including The Supremes, The Temptations, The Marvelettes, The Four Tops, Martha Reeves and The Vandellas, Smokey Robinson and The Miracles, Gladys Knight and The Pips, The Jackson Five, The Velvelettes, Mary Wells, Diana Ross, Marvin Gaye—AND Tammi Terrell—Stevie Wonder, Brenda Holloway, Edwin Starr, Kim Weston and so many more, who churned out a non-stop string of hits from the 1960s to the 80s. Motown was more than just the sound of Black America. It became the "Sound of Young America®"

Motown owned the 1960s, becoming an integral part of the social and cultural fabric of America. By the end of the '60s, it had placed over 350 songs on the popular music charts. Motown was the most consistently successful American record company in the music industry. Today, that fact may seem obvious. But, at the time, Motown's success was profound. It was revolutionary. Motown and its artists changed the recording industry forever. Motown soon became Detroit's most famous and popular export worldwide—rivaling the products coming out of Ford and General Motors. The music of Motown was every bit as influential as was the music of The Beatles.

Founding Motown in 1959 with an $800.00 loan from his family, Berry Gordy Jr.'s vision was to conquer the world. In the process, he assembled one of the most impressive rosters of artists of any record company. Between 1964 and 1969, The Supremes alone were responsible for a record-setting twelve Number One pop hits, plus an additional seven records that landed in the Top Twenty, selling in excess of sixty million records. Only The Beatles and Elvis Presley sold more records than The Supremes in the 1960s. In the 1970s, The Supremes charted another five Top Twenty records. The Four Tops,

Martha Reeves and The Vandellas, The Temptations, The Miracles, The Marvelettes, Mary Wells, and Marvin Gaye were responsible for more than sixty-five Top Twenty hits. You could see Motown artists on television virtually every week or every other week. You could hear their songs on the radio every hour of every day. They regularly performed around the world—including for kings, queens and presidents.

The company remained a potent force in the entertainment industry for thirty years. Marvin Gaye and Stevie Wonder saw their greatest artistic successes during the 1970s. Diana Ross became a major solo superstar, with six more Number One hits. The Temptations, The Supremes and The Four Tops continued as top sellers. With Motown's move from Detroit to Los Angeles in the late 1960s, Berry Gordy fulfilled yet another aspect of his vision by entering the film industry. Diana Ross earned a Best Actress Academy Award nomination for her role in "Lady Sings The Blues," becoming one of the first African American actresses to be so honored. The theme song from Ross' second film, "Mahogany," was nominated for a Best Song Oscar® in 1976; Stevie Wonder's "I Just Called To Say I Love You," featured in the film "The Woman In Red," was nominated for an Oscar® in 1984.

Motown is forever....

So, sit back, relax, and enjoy this pictorial journey back to the magical—and turbulent—1960s. It was a time when culture, society and politics were changing at a rapid pace. And it was the music of Motown that brought people together in a way never before achieved in popular culture. It didn't matter if you were black or white, rich or poor, young or old...we were ALL listening to, dancing to, and buying the music of Motown. Motown provided the soundtrack for the 1960s.

SPECIAL NOTE: This book is a collection of photos taken by Motown fans throughout the years. Because it is based on available photos from those fans willing to share their collections, not all of Motown's artists are represented here. Most of the photos depict Motown artists today, rather than as they appeared in their heyday.

Chapter One

The Music That Inspired A Generation… And Changed The World

PRIOR TO STARTING MOTOWN RECORDS IN 1959, Berry Gordy, Jr., held a variety of jobs—professional boxer, auto assembly line worker, and songwriter for artists like the great Jackie Wilson. Gordy wrote several hits for Wilson, including "Lonely Teardrops." He soon became frustrated when his efforts on behalf of others reaped little financial reward for himself. Along with a small core of staff, and an incredibly small loan—$800.00—from his family, Gordy began to build an empire in which he had complete control over his own destiny. Perhaps one of Motown's first big hits said it all—Barrett Strong's "Money (That's What I Want.)", written by Gordy.

It wasn't long before Gordy and Motown struck gold and were churning out hit after hit. By 1960, The Miracles landed at Number 2 on the pop charts with "Shop Around." The next year, The Marvelettes provided Motown with its first Number 1 pop hit with "Please Mr. Postman." Mary Wells became Motown's first female superstar by recording more than a half dozen Top Ten hits between 1962 and 1964. Motown was fast becoming more successful than any record company could hope to be. And it was Berry Gordy's skill at attracting strong talent that fueled that success. Everyone wanted to be a part of Motown!

Entering its Golden Era in 1964—when Mary Wells and The Supremes provided Motown with four Number One hits—Gordy set out to conquer the world. Early in 1965, the Tamla-Motown Revue landed in England for a nation-wide tour, and filmed an hour-long special for the "Ready, Steady, Go" television show. The Revue played The Olympia Theatre in Paris. The rest, as they say, is history….

Photo 001

Berry Gordy opened The Motown Record Corporation in a duplex at 2648 West Grand Boulevard. The house contained both the company's administrative offices and recording studios, as well as living quarters upstairs. It was here that hundreds of hits were recorded during the 1960s. It is unbelievable to think of how much hit music was produced in this small house—and the legends that were born there. (Photo by Brad Adams, courtesy of the author)

PHOTO 002

The nickname, "Hitsville U.S.A." was a stroke of marketing genius. In the beginning, that name gave the illusion of success to all who passed by. It soon became a self-fulfilling prophesy. The front picture window of the Studio A building was usually crowded with photographs of Motown's artists, copies of album covers, and records—all reminders that Motown was determined to become a force within the recording industry. (Photo by Brad Adams, courtesy of the author.)

Photo 003

In its early incarnation in the 1980s, this simple sign greeted visitors as they entered the Motown Historical Museum. Admission was a mere $3.00. Gold and platinum records lined the walls—as did unframed photographs held in place with tape. Album covers, sheet music and photographs lined the staircase. But, it was for the opportunity to visit the famed Studio A—and to stand where Motown's biggest stars recorded their greatest hits—that fans made the pilgrimage to Motown. (Courtesy of the author.)

Photo 004

In 1989, Randall Wilson and I made a road trip to Detroit—both to see Mary Wilson perform in the '60s musical, "Beehive," at the Stage West Theatre across the river in Windsor, Ontario, and so that Randy could tour me around the landmarks of the city where he spent much of his childhood. The highlight, of course, was our visit to The Motown Historical Museum. Imagine the thrill of walking into Motown's Studio A, set up exactly as it would have been when The Supremes recorded "Where Did Our Love Go?" You could still see the grooves in the floorboards where the singers stood at their microphones. (Courtesy of Randall Wilson.)

PHOTO 005

In this view of Studio A—famously dubbed "the snake pit"—you can see the musicians' stands set with original sheet music, ready for the next recording session. The Funk Brothers—Motown's in-house studio musicians—created the backing tracks that made The Motown Sound so distinctive. Without the creative genius of the Funk Brothers, there would probably not have been a "Motown Sound." At the time, though, The Funk Brothers did not receive any public recognition. They were simply the studio musicians. It wasn't until the 2002 release of the documentary film, "Standing In The Shadows of Motown," that the guys finally received their due. The award-winning documentary breathed new life into The Funk Brothers, who reunited and began touring under their own name. (Courtesy of the author.)

PHOTO 006

Inside the control booth in Studio A, the record producers controlled the recording sessions to achieve just the right sound mix of instruments, background vocals and lead vocals. Berry Gordy ran Motown similar to the auto assembly line on which he used to work. Every aspect of the recording process went through a strict quality control process. It was not uncommon for the singers and musicians to do multiple takes of the same song until it passed muster. No product was allowed to hit the market until it was perfect. That was one of the key factors contributing to Motown's phenomenal success. (Courtesy of Randall Wilson.)

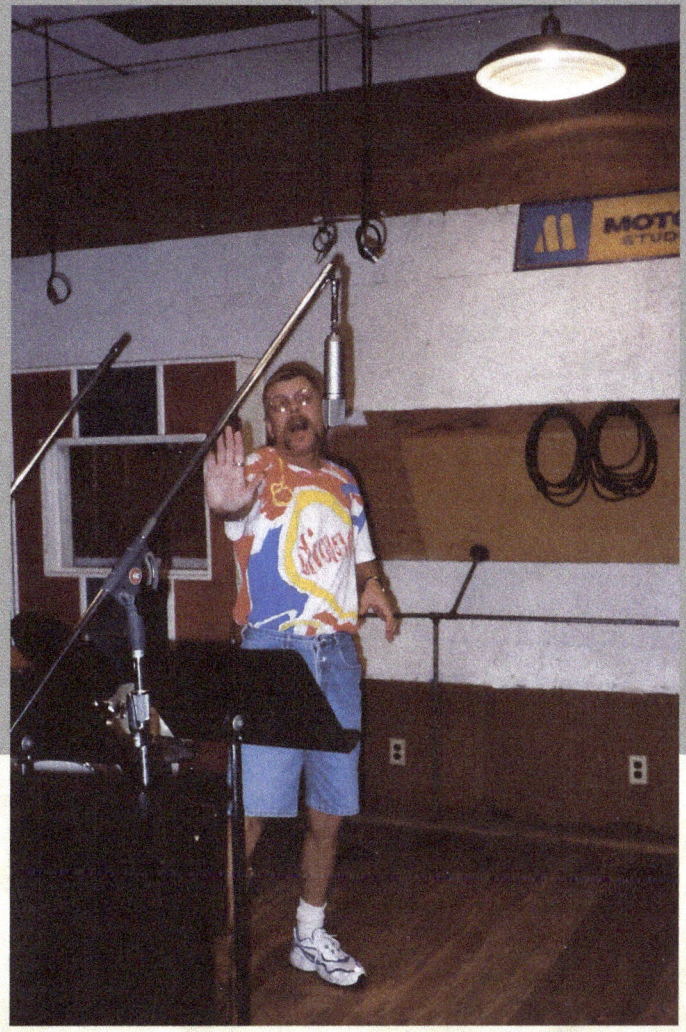

PHOTO 007

In 1996, ardent Motown fan Brad Adams, who lived in Vicksburg, Michigan, fulfilled every Motown fan's dream when he had the opportunity to stand where his idols, The Supremes, stood when they recorded "Stop! In The Name Of Love"— in Studio A. Here, Adams is practicing the distinctive "Stop" hand motion that choreographer Cholly Atkins created for The Supremes. Released in February, 1965, "Stop" became The Supremes' fourth consecutive Number One Song. (Photo by Brad Adams, courtesy of the author.)

Photo 008

This collage of photographs of Motown artists was displayed in Studio A at The Motown Historical Museum, on the wall opposite the musicians' stands. Of course, this is just a fraction of the incredible roster of artists Berry Gordy assembled at Motown. A collage of all the artists would, most likely, stretch for a full city block! Pictured here are Gladys Knight and The Pips, The Four Tops, The Temptations, The Supremes, Lionel Richie, Stevie Wonder, Mary Wells, The Jackson Five, Smokey Robinson and The Miracles, Martha Reeves and The Vandellas, and Marvin Gaye. (Photographer unknown, courtesy of the author.)

PHOTO 009
In October, 1989, Mary Wilson starred in a production of the 60s musical, "Beehive," at the Stage West Theatre in Windsor, Canada. During her stay in the Detroit-area, Wilson visited The Motown Historical Museum for the first time, and took Randy Wilson and I along. Here, Wilson is seen standing on the steps of The Motown Historical Museum during our visit. Behind her is the famed picture window featuring memorabilia from Motown' glory days. (Courtesy of the author.)

Photo 010

Before starting her tour, Mary Wilson was interviewed by a reporter for a local media outlet outside the Museum. Ever the star, Wilson displays the elegance and glamor for which The Supremes became known. Behind the venetian blinds, you also can see museum staff members waiting in anticipation for Wilson entrance into the museum. (Courtesy of Randall Wilson.)

Photo 011
Of course, Mary Wilson wanted to revisit Studio A, where she, Diana Ross, Florence Ballard, and later, Cindy Birdsong recorded some of the most memorable songs in music history—"Baby Love," "I Hear a Symphony," "You Can't Hurry Love," and "Reflections," to name just a few of the group's more than thirty Top Forty hits. Here, she strikes a pose inside Studio A. (Courtesy of the author.)

PHOTO 012 [PREVIOUS PAGE]
I visited the Museum again in 2003, while I was in Detroit with Mary Wilson, who was appearing in "The Vagina Monologues" at the Detroit Opera House. It was a different place. Gone was the somewhat underdeveloped, amateur appearance I had seen during my 1989 tour of the museum, when photographs were literally just taped to the walls. These lavender gowns were designed for The Supremes in 1967. It is not documented whether The Supremes ever really wore this particular set of gowns—although they did wear gowns of identical design, but in silver/blue sequins on a 1967 appearance on television's "The Hollywood Palace." (Courtesy of the author.)

PHOTO 013
In the 1990s and early 2000s, Motown operated a number of Motown Cafes in major cities around the country. In a throwback to the famed MotorTown Revue tours of the early 1960s, tribute groups portraying The Supremes, Martha and The Vandellas, and other Motown artists performed live sets during the hours of operation. The performances were promoted via this representation of a theatre marquee from the 1960s at the New York City Motown Café. (Courtesy of the author.)

PHOTO 014

Capitalizing on the success of the smash Broadway musical, "Dreamgirls," which premiered in 1982, Motown mounted a new marketing campaign to promote albums recorded by The Supremes and Diana Ross. Although the show's creators deny this, it is widely assumed that "Dreamgirls" was loosely based on the story of The Supremes. "Dreamgirls" was made into a feature film in 2005, starring Beyonce and Jennifer Hudson, who won the 2006 Oscar® for Best Supporting Actress for her role as Effie White. During her acceptance speech, Hudson thank The Supremes' Florence Ballard for inspiring her. (Courtesy of the author.)

Chapter Two

The Many Faces of Motown

YOU COULD FILL A WHOLE BOOK with photographs of the dozens of legendary Motown artists. No other record label—before or since—has assembled a roster of performers to match Motown. And that ability to attract so much young, raw and strong talent—as well as his commitment to producing only the highest quality music—was the key to Berry Gordy's success as a producer of popular music.

Of course, everyone is familiar with the megastars of Motown. There are many lesser-known stars, too—those whose creative output was overshadowed by the overwhelming success of groups like The Supremes and The Temptations. Yet, everyone played an important role the history of Motown. While artists like The Andantes, Frances Nero, Bettye LaVette, Kim Weston, Brenda Holloway, and The Velvelettes, may not be as well known as Mary Wells, Marvin Gaye, Stevie Wonder and Martha Reeves and The Vandellas, they none-the-less made contributions of their own. It also is not widely known that artists like 50s pop crooner and actor Tony Martin—who recorded a cover version of The Supremes' "Ask Any Girl" (re-titled, "Ask Any Man".) recorded for Motown. Other artists not commonly associated with The Motown Sound who recorded for the company at one time or another include Lesley Gore, The Four Seasons, Pat Boone, Bruce Willis and Diahann Carroll. Lesley Gore's shimmering 1972 Motown album, "Someplace Else Now," for which she wrote or co-wrote all of the songs—was buried for decades, finally being released on CD in 2015.

There is one thing about all of Motown's artists though—whether they achieved mega-success or remained in the shadows—they continue to perform and come out for entertainment industry events to this day. You see, when you love what you do—and when you have been given a gift—you never lose your that passion to share your life with your audience. Motown has perhaps the most ardent fans of any record label. For Motown fans, this has meant continued access to their favorite performers. Concerts, reunions, fan conventions, induction ceremonies—attend any of these, whether in Detroit, New York, Los Angels, or London—and you are likely to see some of your favorite Motown stars.

PHOTO 015

Saxophone player Autry DeWalt Jr. got his nickname, "Walker," because he didn't own a car and walked everywhere. Jr. Walker brought a new element to Motown's roster—a singer who also was an instrumentalist. His group, Jr. Walker and The All Stars hit it big in 1965 with their signature song, "Shotgun." The group produced a number of hits, including "I'm A Road Runner," and "What Does It Take (To Win Your Love.)." Here, Walker is seen in the Motown recording studio—"the snake pit"—during an early recording session. (Photographer unknown; photo provided by Peter Benjaminson.)

Photo 016

Jr. Walker certainly could blow on that sax! In addition to original recordings written specifically for him, Jr. Walker and his group also scored hits with best-selling covers of The Supremes' "Come See About Me," and Marvin Gaye's "How Sweet It Is (To Be Loved By You)." (Photographer unknown; photo supplied by Peter Benjaminson.)

PHOTO 017

Ask any former Motown artist, and they will tell you that working at Motown was like being part of a big family. And in March of 2003, Mary Wilson returned to Detroit to star in "The Vagina Monologues" at The Opera House. Her Motown family turned out in force! Here, Wilson is pictured with Maxine Powell—who ran Motown's Artist Development Department—and Rosalind Ashford, Annette Helton, and Martha Reeves, of Martha and The Vandellas. (Courtesy of the author.)

PHOTO 018

During her run in "The Vagina Monologues," Wilson celebrated her birthday with a party at Bert's on Broadway. In attendance were members of The Andantes, The Miracles, songwriter Ivy Joe Hunter, and many of Wilson's childhood friends and classmates. Here, Wilson shares a moment with Martha Reeves, and Motown producer Johnny Bristol. Bristol produced Diana Ross and The Supremes' last Number One song of the 1960s, "Someday We'll Be Together,' in 1969—on which his voice can be heard. Martha Reeves is one of the few Motown artists who never left Detroit. She continues to live in the city, and several years ago was elected to a term on the Detroit City Council. (Courtesy of the author.)

PHOTO 019

At Bert's On Broadway, a luminous Mary Wilson poses with members of The Miracles, including Bobby Rogers—the only original member still with the group. When Smokey Robinson left The Miracles in the early 1970s, he was replaced by Billy Griffin. The Miracles went on to score several more major hits, including the Number One hit, "Love Machine" in 1975. Over the years, a number of different singers have joined the group. In addition to Rogers, Dave Finley and former Motown arranger Paul Riser helped Wilson celebrate her birthday. (Courtesy of the author.)

Photo 020

Among those helping Wilson to celebrate her birthday at Bert's On Broadway were some of her classmates from Northeastern High School. Wilson and Florence Ballard both attended Northeastern, while Diana Ross attended Cass Technical High School. Ballard and Wilson became friends when they performed at a talent show at school—telling each other that if anyone contacted them about forming a singing group, they would remember each other. Several weeks later, when The Primes approached Florence Ballard about forming a girl group, and asked if she knew anyone else, she responded, "my friend Mary...." They then asked a girl who lived in the neighborhood to join them—Diane Ross. One of The Primes knew another young singer—Betty McGlown. And the quartet known as The Primettes was born. When The Primettes first auditioned for Berry Gordy in 1960, he told them to come back after they finished high school. Imagine going to school with future superstars! (Courtesy of the author.)

PHOTO 021

Conventions allow both Motown performers and their fans to interact on a more intimate level. One such event was held in 1998—a Motown fan convention at The Motown Café in New York City. Attending were Scherrie Payne and Lynda Laurence of The Supremes, Betty Kelly of Martha and The Vandellas, Frances Nero, and others. Betty Kelly joined Martha and The Vandellas in 1964, replacing Annette Sterling. Prior to becoming a Vandella, Kelly had been a member of another Motown girl group, The Velvelettes. It was not uncommon for members of one group to jump ship and join another group when an opportunity arose. Seen here at the Motown convention, Betty Kelly poses with Barbara Combes Ingrassia, who displays her finest Motown diva red sequins! (Courtesy of the author.)

PHOTO 022
Motown's artists attracted a worldwide audience never before reached by African American performers. Among those attending the 1998 Motown Convention was Ulf Wahlberg—who traveled from Stockholm, Sweden to meet some of the artists he grew up listening to, including Frances Nero. Although not one of Motown's better-known artists in America, Nero is a beloved artist on the British Northern Soul circuit. Her most recognized song is ""Keep On Lovin' Me." Wahlberg is an expert on Motown in Sweden, and maintains an extensive collection of Motown memorabilia. (Courtesy of Ulf Wahlberg.)

Photo 023

Detroit-native Scherrie Payne attended Michigan State University and Wayne State University, where she earned a teaching certificate. Scherrie and her sister—Freda Payne—both recorded for Detroit-based Invictus Records, founded by Holland-Dozier-Holland, after H-D-H left Motown in 1968 over a contract dispute. In 1973, Mary Wilson invited Payne to join The Supremes when she was looking for a singer to replace the recently-departed lead singer, Jean Terrell. A talented singer, songwriter and playright, Payne is pictured here at the Motown Convention with Swedish fan Ulf Wahlberg, and Barbara Combes Ingrassia. (Courtesy of Ulf Wahlberg.)

Photo 024

The Supremes' gowns are almost as famous as the group! Their stage costumes were created for them by the top designers of the day, including Michael Travis and Bob Mackie. Mary Wilson has maintained many of these legendary gowns, which travel the world as a museum exhibition. Here, Ulf Wahlberg poses with two of the gowns from the collection, which Wilson loaned for display at the 1998 Motown Convention. The gown to the left was worn by The Supremes during a 1968 Command Performance before the British royal family. Encrusted with hundreds of rhinestones, sequins and beads sewn onto pink velvet fabric, these gowns weigh close to thirty pounds each! Imagine performing in these costumes under hot stage lights… and making it look easy! (Courtesy of Ulf Wahlberg.)

Photo 025

In the late 1980s, British record producer Ian Levine formed Motor City Records, gathering together dozens of former Motown artists, sparking a resurgence of interest in Motown music in England—and revitalizing the recording careers of the artists. Tours featured The Former Ladies of The Supremes, Martha and The Vandellas, The Commodores, Kim Weston, Brenda Holloway, and others. Pictured here while on tour in England in 1995 are members of The Commodores and Former Ladies of The Supremes—Scherrie Payne and Lynda Laurence, with Lynda's sister, Sundray Tucker, who joined FLOS when Jean Terrell left. Interestingly, when The Supremes were looking for a replacement for group member Cindy Birdsong in late 1971, they were first interested in Tucker—who, along with her sister, was performing as a member of Stevie Wonder's backing group, WonderLove. After watching a performance, however, The Supremes offered Lynda the opportunity to join the legendary group. (Photo by the late Jonathan Ptak. Courtesy of the author.)

PHOTO 026

Concerts featuring Motown artists are very popular during pledge drives on PBS. I was very fortunate to have been involved with the taping of two such specials. One such concert was filmed in 2002 in Pittsburgh, featuring Dennis Edwards' Temptations Review, Johnny Bristol, Thelma Houston, The Originals and The Andantes, and co-hosted by Mary Wilson, Aretha Franklin, and Lou Rawls. Many of these artists had not performed on the same stage with each other in years. Between sets, Mary Wilson took a few moments to catch up with Johnny Bristol—a Motown producer and singer in his own right ("Hang On In There Baby") and Billy Paul—whose "Me and Mrs. Jones" is a classic. (Courtesy of the author.)

PHOTO 027

The Originals started at Motown as the in-house male backup group. Their voices can be heard on hundreds of songs. By the late 1960s, however, they were front and center with hits of their own—"Baby I'm For Real," and "The Bells," and the disco classic "Going Down to Love Town." The Originals were part of the 2002 taping of the PBS concert special. In this photograph, they are seen in the rehearsal hall on the day before the concert taping. (Courtesy of the author.)

Photo 028

The early 1960s was the golden era of the Girl Groups. In 2003, Mary Wilson launched a project to honor twelve of the legendary Girl Groups from the 1960s with postage stamps issued by two African and three Caribbean nations, under the direction of the International Philatelic Society. Featuring portraits of The Angels, The Chantels, The Cookies, The Crystals, The Dixie Cups, Patti LaBelle and The Bluebelles, The Marvelettes, Martha Reeves and The Vandellas, The Ronettes, The Shirelles, The Supremes, and The Velvelettes created by the artist Yemi, the stamps were unveiled during a lavish ceremony at the Rock and Roll Hall of Fame and Museum. The ceremony and concert that followed brought together thirty-three members of these twelve groups, and attracted an audience of over 1200 fans—the largest audience for a Rock Hall event up to that time. It was the first time in history that all of these singers had shared the same stage. Many had not even seen each other in decades. Here, Martha Reeves, Rosalind Ashford and Annette Helton entertain their friends at a private party the evening before the ceremony, with a rousing rendition of their signature song, "Dancing In The Street." (Courtesy of the author.)

PHOTO 029

2004 saw Mary Wilson back at the Rock Hall to unveil the inaugural exhibition of "The Mary Wilson Supremes Gown Collection." As the only member of The Supremes to remain in the group from beginning to end, Mary saved all of the gorgeous—and legendary—stage costumes for which the group was famous. For the past decade, the gown collection has traveled the world, including exhibitions in England, Russia, and throughout the United States. Joining her for the gala were Rosalind Ashford and Annette Helton of The Vandellas, and Mrs. Maxine Powell, who ran Motown's famous Artist Development Department in the 1960s. During a break in rehearsals, Ashford, Helton, and Mrs. Powell took time to pose with the Rock Hall's Ruthie Brown (center). (Courtesy of the author.)

Photo 030 [left]
Before joining the Motown family in the early 1960s, the late Maxine Powell ran a modeling agency in Detroit. Berry Gordy hired her to run his Artist Development Department—Motown's charm school. All of Motown's artists were required to attend Mrs. Powell's classes before they were sent out on the road. Under her tutelage, young singers learned how to be stars. Referring to them as "diamonds in the rough," she said that one day, they would perform before kings and queens. And so they did! Throughout her life, Mrs. Powell continued to tutor young people through her motivational programs. (Courtesy Rusty Maghanoy.)

Photo 031
The Velvelettes never achieved the success of The Marvelettes, Martha and The Vandellas, or The Supremes. But, they hold a distinction the other groups cannot claim. They are the only group today performing with four original members—Caldin (Carolyn) Gill Street, Mildred Gill Arbor, Norma Barbee Fairhurst, and Bertha Barbee McNeil. Bertha and Mildred founded the group while they were students at Western Michigan University. Milly and Cal are sisters. Norma and Bertha are cousins. Betty Kelly rounded out the original quintet. In 1964, Kelly was pulled from The Velvelettes to replace Annette Sterling, who was leaving Martha and The Vandellas. Another former member of The Velvelettes—Sandra Tilly—also left the group to join Martha and The Vandellas in the late 1960s. Today, The Velvelettes continue to thrill fans both in the United States and in Europe. Their hits include "He Was Really Saying Something," and "Needle In A Haystack." Here, The Velvelettes are pictured before an outdoor concert in Maryland in 2005. (Courtesy of the author.)

Photo 032
Another venue that has brought Motown artists together in recent years is the Vocal Group Hall of Fame. In 2003, The Temptations, under the leadership of Otis Williams—the sole surviving original member—performed at the Hall's Induction Ceremony concert. The Temptations are one of the few groups that have been able to succeed through numerous personnel changes over the years. Perhaps the reason for this stems from the fact that there was no one designated lead singer. In their early days, David Ruffin, Eddie Kendricks and Paul Williams each sang lead on the group's recordings. When Ruffin left The Temptations to pursue a solo career in 1967, he was replaced by Dennis Edwards. Between 1964 and 1986, The Temptations charted an incredible thirty Top Forty pop hits—including their signature song, "My Girl," "Get Ready," "Ain't Too Proud To Beg," "Cloud Nine," and "Papa was A Rolling Stone." (Courtesy of the author.)

Photo 033

In 2002, Mary Wilson inducted her label-mates, The Four Tops, into the Vocal Group Hall of Fame. The Four Tops had a long and successful career at Motown, charting 28 singles, including two that went all the way to Number One—"I Can't Help Myself (Sugar Pie Honey Bunch.)," and "Reach Out, I'll Be There." In 1972, The Four Tops left Motown for Dunhill Records (and later, ABC Records and Casablanca Records), charting an additional 16 singles. In this photograph, Abdul "Duke" Fakir, the Tops sole surviving original member, accepts his award from Wilson. (Courtesy of the author.)

Photo 034

You can tell by their smiles that Mary Wilson and Duke Fakir share a special bond. In the 1970s, The Supremes and The Four Tops recorded three albums together, and were dubbed "The Magnificent Seven" by Motown. Their biggest single together—a remake of Ike and Tina Turner's "River Deep Mountain High"—reached Number 14 on the pop charts. Their version blew Ike and Tina's version—which was written by Phil Spector, Jeff Barry and Ellie Greenwich, and produced by Spector—out of the water. The original version peaked at Number Sixty-Six on the pop charts. Prior to accepting his trophy from the Vocal Group Hall of Fame, Fakir takes time to pose with Wilson. (Courtesy of the author.)

Photo 035

This photo says so much about the bonds that the artists from the 1950s and 1960s share. Mary Wilson is inducting members of The Drifters—the late Bill Pinkney, the late Ben E. King, and Charlie Thomas—into the Vocal Group Hall of Fame. To the right is author Joel Whitburn, whose books based on the *Billboard* music charts are considered Bibles in the music industry. These seminal artists opened the doors for the artists who followed. (Courtesy of the author).

PHOTO 036

The Rhythm and Blues Foundation also brings together legendary artists from the 1960s, recognizing their seminal contributions to music, culture and society—contributions that often are overlooked or ignored by other organizations. In 2003, The Supremes were among the inductees. Here, Mary Wilson shares a laugh with Bettye LaVette, and pop superstar Bonnie Raitt before the induction ceremonies. Long before she became a jazz sensation, LaVette briefly recorded for Motown Records. (Courtesy of the author.)

PHOTO 037

Also on hand to accept their late mother's Rhythm and Blues award were Florence Ballard's three daughters—Lisa, Michelle, and Nicole Chapman. Ballard's daughters were still very young children when their mother passed away at age 32, in 1976. During the awards ceremony, Mary Wilson brought Lisa, Michelle, and Nicole on stage, introducing them to the audience and paying tribute to their mother's contributions to The Supremes. (Courtesy of the author.)

Photo 038

In 1987, the Whitney Gallery in Los Angeles mounted an exhibition honoring Florence Ballard's life and career, organized by Allen White, then president of The Florence Ballard Fan Club. Attending the opening were were Mary Wilson, Scherrie Payne, Gladys Horton, Lisa Chapman, and Fuller Gordy. Also in attendance was singer Carolyn Willis. Willis' group, Honeycone, recorded for Holland-Dozier-Holland's Detroit-based Invictus Records in the 1970s, for which Scherrie Payne also recorded as part of the group Glass House. Honeycone's hits included "Want Ads," "One Monkey Don't Stop No Show," and "Sitting On A Time Bomb (Waiting For The Hurt To Come.) Shown here at the exhibit opening, Carolyn Willis shares a laugh with Scherrie Payne—who joined The Supremes in 1973. (Courtesy of the author.)

Photo 039

Soupy Sales is best known as a comedian and children's television show host. His slapstick comedy kept people laughing throughout the 1960s. What many people forget is that he was also a Motown recording artist! Following on the success of his novelty single, "The Mouse," Sales signed with Motown in 1969, recording a novelty single, "Muck-Arty Park" (a play on "Macarthur Park"), and album, "A Bag of Soup." Here, Sales is seen with Mary Wilson at a 2001 fan convention and meet and greet. (Courtesy of the author.)

PHOTO 040
Fan conventions and expos bring together stars from all segments of the entertainment industry. The artists sell their merchandise and sign autographs, while the fans have the opportunity to meet and greet their favorite stars "up close and personal." Mary Wilson and actor LaVar Burton share a moment at one such convention where they both appeared. (Courtesy of the author.)

PHOTO 041 [NEXT PAGE]
The Temptations have undergone many changes in their lineup over the years. The one constant has been Otis Williams, who was there at the beginning and continues to perform with the group today. Before coming together as The Temptations in the early 1960s, Williams had his own group—Otis Williams and The Distants (which also included original Temptation Melvin Franklin, and future Temptation Richard Street). Eddie Kendricks and Paul Williams were members of a group called The Primes. When The Primes were looking to form a sister group to perform with them—to be dubbed The Primettes—they approached a teenaged Florence Ballard, who recruited her friend Mary Wilson. They asked a girl they knew from their neighborhood—Diane Ross. Another young singer, Betty McGlown, joined to complete the quartet. The rest, as they say, is history. The Primes and The Distants merged to form The Temptations, and The Primettes became The Supremes when they signed with Motown Records in early 1961. The two groups—by now superstars—would reunite on a 1967 episode of "The Ed Sullivan Show," singing a medley of each others' hits. The success of that appearance led Motown to pair the two groups in the recording studio for two albums, as well as two highly rated NBC-TV specials in 1968 and 1969. The pairing produced the Number Two pop hit, "I'm Gonna Make You Love Me." Here, a latter-day edition of The Temptations performs live on stage. Pictured are Harry McGilberry, Barrington (Bo) Henderson, Otis Williams, Ron Tyson, and Terry Weeks. (Courtesy Dan and Marie Leighton.)

Chapter Three

Motown and Detroit

MOTOWN ENCOMPASSED much more than just the duplex it occupied at 2648 West Grand Boulevard. It was an integral part of the whole city. Before its artists started performing at posh supper clubs, theaters and arenas around the world, they performed at area clubs, including the 20 Grand, the Roostertail, the Graystone Ballroom—where Berry Gordy held the company's annual Christmas party during the early years—the Flame Show Bar, Cobo Hall, the Fox Theater, the Detroit Opera House. Martha Reeves was discovered by Mickey Stevenson at the 20 Grand. That is how it happened for many of the youngsters coming to Motown.

They came—these young singers eager for stardom—from the street corners and neighborhoods of the city. From the Brewster-Douglass Housing Projects. They heard that Motown was THE place to be if you wanted to record. As their fortunes increased, they bought homes in neighborhoods like Buena Vista and Boston Boulevard—site of the so-called Motown Mansion, owned by Berry Gordy.

As the company grew and its success spread, Motown needed more space. In 1968, it moved to the much larger Donovan Building at 2457 Woodward Avenue, where it remained until the company's move to Los Angeles was completed in 1972.

Even venerable venues like Orchestra Hall and the Art Institute played significant roles in the history of Motown, as we shall see.

Motown's move to Los Angeles in 1972 left a void in the city. It also left behind many of the artists who had helped to build Motown's success in the early 1960s. Although some recording continued to take place in Detroit in the early 1970s, recording operations began shifting to Los Angeles as early as the late 1960s. Yet, the company and the city remain intimately connected. Motown and Detroit will be forever linked—no matter where the music itself is made. The renaissance and expansion of The Motown Historical Museum has brought new life to Motown's place of honor in the city of Detroit.

Photo 042

In the 1980s, The Motown Historical Museum was declared a Michigan Historic Site, designated with this historic marker. As noted, the company was originally known as Tamla Records. When he was getting ready to incorporate the company in early 1960, Gordy decided to choose a new name that reflected its geographic location. Motown actually was a group of four labels—Motown, Gordy, Tamla and Soul. In the early 1970s—reflecting its move to the West Coast—the short-lived MoWest label was added. From these humble beginning on West Grand Boulevard, Motown provided an opportunity for Detroit's inner city youth to live into their dreams. (Courtesy of Randall Wilson.)

Photo 043

The Supremes came to Motown in 1960 from their families' homes in the Brewster-Douglass Housing Projects. In the fall of 1965, following their successful—and groundbreaking—concert at Avery Fisher Hall at New York's Lincoln Center, The Supremes returned to Detroit and visited their former neighborhood. In this *Detroit News* photograph, they are seen walking through the Projects, waving to their many fans. The Supremes had moved out of the Projects just a few months before—buying houses for themselves and their families. How far they had come! (Courtesy of *The Detroit News*.)

Photo 044

Named after African American abolitionist Fredrick Douglass, the Brewster-Douglass Housing Projects were the largest residential housing project in Detroit, begun in 1935, with First Lady Eleanor Roosevelt breaking ground. By 1941, there were close to 1000 housing units in the Projects. The Projects were again expanded between 1952 and 1955, with the addition of six 14-story high rise buildings. At its peak, it housed upwards of 10,000 residents. The Projects were located in the Brush Park section of east Detroit, near the Chrysler Freeway, Mack Avenue and St. Antoine Street. They were built to house Detroit's "working poor." By the 1970s, the Projects had begun to deteriorate, with one section being converted to housing for senior citizens. In addition to Diana Ross, Mary Wilson and Florence Ballard, the Projects were also home to Lily Tomlin. Scenes for the film version of *Dreamgirls* were filmed in the Projects, and the children's claymation television series, *The PJs*, was based on the Brewster-Douglass Projects. What remained of the Projects is seen here in March of 2003. (Courtesy of the author.)

PHOTO 045 [LEFT]
Demolition of The Brewster Projects began in 1991 and continued until 2008. Knowing that her childhood home at 1200 St. Antoine was in the process of being demolished, Mary Wilson took the opportunity to visit the Projects one last time in March, 2003, when she was in the city for a week-long turn starring in "The Vagina Monologues." It was in the Projects that the nucleus of The Supremes was formed. Florence Ballard and Mary Wilson had met at school, when they both performed at a talent show. They vowed that if either was approached about joining a group, she would remember the other. A few weeks later, Ballard was approached by a local male vocal group, The Primes, about forming a "sister group." She asked Wilson to join. Another girl they knew from the Projects—Diane Ross—joined, along with a fourth girl, Betty McGlown. They called themselves The Primettes., and sang at talent shows and sock hops. The Primettes thought they had made it when, in July of 1960, they took first place in an amateur contest at the Detroit/Windsor Freedom Festival—winning a cash prize of $15.00! Here, Wilson is seen standing in front of the gutted remains of the building she grew up in. (Courtesy of the author.)

THE GOLD CADILLAC FLORENCE GOT AFTER LEAVING THE SUPREMES STILL DOMINATED THE DRIVEWAY OF HER BUENA VISTA HOME ON THIS COLD DECEMBER DAY IN 1970.

(photo courtesy of Randall Wilson December 3, 1970)

Photo 046 [left]
By 1965, The Supremes were on top of the world. They had five consecutive Number One records—"Where Did Our Love Go,' "Baby Love," "Come See About Me," "Stop In The Name of Love," and "Back In My Arms Again." They had been to Europe twice. They had appeared on "The Ed Sullivan Show," "The Hollywood Palace," Dean Martin's and Red Skelton's television variety shows. They had appeared in the theatrical film "Beach Ball," and the concert film, "Teenage Music International." They were on the cover of *Ebony* and *Time* magazines. They had just performed a concert at Lincoln Center in New York. Success! Now it was time to enjoy some of the fruits of their efforts. Despite the fact that they traveled constantly and did not spend much time in Detroit, Diana Ross, Mary Wilson, and Florence Ballard each bought themselves homes in the city—and they also moved their families out of the Projects. Ballard purchased this stately Tudor-style house on Buena Vista. In this 1970 photo of Ballard's Buena Vista home, you can see the gold Cadillac she purchased with a portion of the settlement money she received when she left The Supremes, sitting in the driveway. Sadly, Ballard lost her home to foreclosure after she was unable to launch a solo career. (Courtesy of Randall Wilson.)

Photo 047

The Detroit Institute of Arts formed the backdrop for this dramatic picture of The Four Tops in 1966. Founded in 1885 and originally located on Jefferson Avenue, the Institute moved to a larger facility on Woodward Avenue in 1927—affectionately referred to as the "temple of art." Today, the DIA's collection is classified as one of the six best in the United States, spanning from prehistoric times up to the 21st century. (Photographer unknown; courtesy of Peter Benjaminson.)

Photo 048 [RIGHT]

In another scene from the Institute of Arts photo shoot, The Four Tops strike a serious pose with a sculpture of The Thinker. The Four Tops had been together for almost ten years when they signed with Motown in 1963. Their first Motown release, "Baby I Need Your Loving," sailed all the way to Number 11 on the pop charts. Billboard magazine—the Bible of the music industry—named "I Can't Help Myself"—which replaced The Supremes' "Back In My Arms Again" at Number One the week of June 19, 1965— its Record of the Year in 1965. The group hit the top of the charts again in 1966 with "Reach Out, I'll Be There." (Photographer unknown; courtesy of Peter Benjaminson.)

PHOTO 049 [PREVIOUS PAGE]
By 1968, Motown was rapidly outgrowing its headquarters on West Grand Boulevard. In that year, the company moved its administrative operations to the Donovan Building, located at 2457 Woodward Avenue. Built in 1922, Motown occupied the building until 1972, when it moved its operations to the West Coast. The building was closed in 1974, and it was finally demolished in 2006, to make room for a parking lot for visitors coming to Detroit for that year's Super Bowl. (Photo by Karl Wellman, courtesy of Peter Benjaminson.)

PHOTO 050
Motown continued to operate out of both buildings until 1972—surviving the riots that rocked Detroit during the late 1960s. By 1968, Motown faced criticism from black power advocates because its music did not reflect the times. In 1967, Black Panther leader H. Rap Brown famously said, "The name of the game is an eye for an eye, a tooth for a tooth, a life for a life. And Motown, if you don't come around, we are going to burn you down." And by the late 1960s, Motown did begin to change its sound to reflect the times, with songs whose lyrics touched on politics, race and society—including The Temptations' "Cloud Nine," "Ball of Confusion (That's What The World Is Today," and "Runaway Child, Running Wild;" Martha Reeves and The Vandellas' "I Should be Proud;" The Four Tops' "What Is A Man," and "A Simple Game;" Edwin Starr's "War;" Marvin Gaye's seminal "What's Going On;" "Inner City Blues (Make Me Want To Holler;" and Diana Ross and The Supremes' "Love Child," "I'm Living In Shame," and "Shadows of Society." (Photo by Karl Wellman, courtesy of Peter Benjaminson.)

Photo 051

One might wonder how Motown and the Detroit Symphony Orchestra could possibly be connected. Listen to the instrumental tracks to Motown's greatest hits and you have your answer. While The Funk Brothers provided the rhythm tracks to songs like "I Could Never Love Another After Loving You," "Honey Chile," "I Hear A Symphony," and "Reflections," Berry Gordy called upon musicians from the Detroit Symphony Orchestra to add the strings that gave depth, drama and that full sound rarely heard on other recordings at the time. Built in 1919 for the Detroit Symphony—which was then housed at the Greystone Ballroom—it was an acoustical wonder. The Symphony stayed at Orchestra Hall until 1938 when it moved to the Masonic Temple. After that, the building went into receivership, later becoming the Paradise Theater. The Paradise closed in the late 1940s. The building was scheduled for demolition in 1970, when members of the Orchestra formed a fund raising group to save it. The Detroit Symphony Orchestra moved back to Orchestra Hall in the late 1980s—making this a Detroit success story! (Courtesy of Randall Wilson.)

PHOTO 052 [LEFT]
Opened in 1922, the Detroit Opera House was originally known as the Capitol Theatre. Located at 1526 Broadway Street in downtown Detroit, the Opera House sits within the Grand Circus Park Historic District. When it opened, it was said to be the fifth largest movie theatre in the world. As was the case with many movie houses at the time, live entertainment was presented as well as feature films. Jazz legends such as Duke Ellington and Louis Armstrong performed there. A series of name changes followed, including the Paramount Theater and the Broadway Capitol Theater, and finally the Grand Circus Theatre. The theatre closed in 1978. The Michigan Opera Theatre purchased the building in 1988, renaming it the Detroit Opera House. Luciano Pavarotti opened the newly restored Opera House with a gala concert in 1996. In 2003, Mary Wilson starred in a week-long run of "The Vagina Monologues" at the Opera House, bringing a touch of Motown magic to the elegant venue. In 2005, The Four Tops celebrated their fiftieth anniversary in show business with a gala concert at the Opera House, featuring Mary Wilson, Nick Ashford and Valerie Simpson, The Temptations Review featuring Dennis Edwards, Paul Rodgers, and Aretha Franklin, which was filmed for DVD release. Pictured here is the Opera House's lobby as it appeared at the time. (Courtesy of the author.)

Photo 053

This stately home at 918 West Boston Boulevard is now known as the "Motown Mansion." Berry Gordy purchased the mansion in 1967, becoming its fourth owner. He retained ownership of the mansion until 2002, when he sold it to Cynthia F. Reaves—who grew up across the street from the mansion and remembers seeing all of the glamorous, star-studded parties held there. Over the years, the mansion played host to the likes of The Supremes, Stevie Wonder, The Marvelettes, Martha and The Vandellas, The Temptations and The Four Tops, Kim Weston, The Jackson Five, Esther Gordy Edwards, and more. They would jam around the piano, and play billiards in the pool room. Built in 1917 by Danish businessman Nels Michelson, the home has been owned at various times by L.A. Young—who purchased it from Michelson in 1925, and Pablo Davis, who purchased it from Young. Davis was an artist who worked with Diego Rivera on the famed Detroit Industry Mural at the Detroit Institute of Arts. It was recently reported that the mansion is again on the market. (Courtesy of Alexander Atwell.)

PHOTO 054

The Upper Deck at The Roostertail—Detroit's premier nightclub—played an integral part in Motown's growing success in the 1960s. It was famous for its "Motown Mondays," often hosted by DJ Scott Regen—when Motown artists would perform live for appreciative hometown audiences. In 1966, Motown released a series of Live albums recorded at The Roostertail—including concerts by The Four Tops, The Temptations, and Martha Reeves and The Vandellas. The Supremes also recorded a Live album at The Roostertail in 1966, which went unreleased until it was included in the 2012 expanded edition CD release of the group's 1966 studio album, "I Hear A Symphony." Live tracks recorded by Tammi Terrell at The Roostertail also were released as part of the 2010 CD, "Tammi Terrell: Come On and See Me—The Complete Solo Collection." (Courtesy Dan and Marie Leighton)

Chapter Four

The Supreme Dream

ELEGANCE, GLITTER AND TALENT—mixed with a sassy earthiness—made The Supremes unforgettable in performance and kept crowds cheering for seventeen years—from 1961 to 1977, when the group disbanded. The Supremes had a long run at the top, longer than most groups. They charted an unprecedented twelve Number One singles between 1964 and 1969, selling in excess of sixty million units—a sales figure previously unheard of for African American artists...especially women. They were trendsetters who helped to break down racial, social and gender barriers, opening the doors for the artists who would follow. The Supremes were the first female group to chart a Number One album on the *Billboard* charts—"The Supremes A Go-Go" in 1966. They endorsed Coca-Cola® and Arrid Extra Dry Deodorant before it was in vogue for celebrities to do product endorsements. Diana Ross, Mary Wilson, and Florence Ballard—three young African American women from Detroit's Brewster-Douglass Housing Projects—were the top selling American act of the 1960s. They were more successful than any group could hope to be. The Supremes were the jewels in the Motown crown. They were Detroit's most well-known exports, bringing The Motown Sound to audiences around the world. In the process, they became "America's Sweethearts."

I grew up with The Supremes. Don't misunderstand—I wasn't raised in Detroit's Brewster-Douglass Housing Projects. And, for sure, The Supremes didn't live in tiny Middletown, New York! No—our cultural and physical neighborhoods were hundreds of miles and a world apart. But, in 1964—just as I was becoming aware of the music playing on the radio—Diana, Mary and Flo—the legendary Supremes—burst into the American musical consciousness with their first chart-topper.

In fact, I will never that summer of 1964, because that is when my dream was born. I was lying on the beach in Sea Bright, New Jersey, when all of a sudden I heard the most exquisite sound coming out of my ever-present transistor radio. It was The Supremes' "Where Did Our Love Go?" I was in love—head over heels in love—and my life changed forever that day. From that moment on, I could literally trace my life through the music of The Supremes and Motown. It formed the soundtrack to my life.

And then it happened. December 27, 1964. I was watching "The Ed Sullivan Show," as we all did in the 1960s, right? And there they were, right in my living room. These three goddesses whom I idolized. I remember as if it was yesterday turning to my mother and saying, "I'm gonna meet them someday!" Yeah, right. I'm eleven years old and living in a small town in upstate New York. What did I know about meeting celebrities? But that performance moved something inside of me, inspiring me to dream.

I DID end up meeting The Supremes. Just eight years after saying that to my mother, when I was a nineteen-year old college student, I interviewed Mary Wilson for an article I had written. Today, I trace all that I have accomplished in life to that night in December, 1964. I had the great privilege of working for Mary Wilson for several years, and also worked with The Velvelettes for a time. I host a weekly, three-hour radio show, "The Motown Jukebox," on WCUW 91.3FM in Worcester, Massachusetts. I travel the country with the lecture programs, "Motown and The Civil Rights Movement," and "Girl Power: The Supremes as Cultural Icons." And it all started with the music coming out of a little transistor radio. You see, you never know where you will find your inspiration. As The Supremes sang in their 1967 Number One hit, "It happened to me, and it can happen to you."

In all, there have been only eight women who were officially members of The Supremes: Barbara Martin, Diana Ross, Mary Wilson, Florence Ballard, Cindy Birdsong (who replaced Ballard in 1967.), Jean Terrell (who replaced Ross in 1970.), Lynda Laurence (who replaced Birdsong in 1972; Birdsong returned to the group in 1973.), Scherrie Payne (who replaced Terrell in 1973.), and Susaye Greene (who replaced Birdsong in 1976.). Through its history, Mary Wilson was the group's one constant.

PHOTOS 055, 056, 057 [FOLLOWING PAGES]
After signing with Motown in January of 1961, The Supremes were anything but an overnight success. They became known as the "No-Hit Supremes." While other acts were scoring hits, The Supremes' first eight recordings were all flops. On tours, they were the opening act. Hard Work finally paid off in 1964, when The Supremes were paired with Holland-Dozier-Holland to record a song written for The Marvelettes—that The Marvelettes rejected. The Supremes didn't like the song, either. But they were not in a position to turn it down. Recording it was the best thing that could have happened to them. During the summer of 1964, while The Supremes were the opening act on Dick Clark's Caravan of Stars tour, "Where Did Our Love Go" climbed the charts. Its softly sensual, repetitive beat clicked with record buyers and radio programmers. The song hit Number One on August 17—and The Supremes became the headliners on the Dick Clark tour. By 1965, The Supremes became the only American group in history to chart five consecutive Number One songs in less than a year. In these photographs, the "No-Hit Supremes" are seen backstage at Washington's Howard Theatre in 1963. (Photographer unknown; photos provided by Sharon Moore.)

Reflections of a Love Supreme

Reflections of a Love Supreme

PHOTO 058

In the same way The Beatles took America by storm, Motown became the rage in England. When "Baby Love" went to Number One in England, Motown sent The Supremes on their first British tour in 1964. They returned to Europe in 1965 with the Tamla-Motown tour. Not bad for three young women from the Projects, who were virtually unknown just a few months before. In this 1965 photograph, Florence Ballard and Mary Wilson are seen arriving in Paris. (Photographer unknown, from the author's collection.)

PHOTO 059

Known for their elegance and style—even when they were making their own, home-made stage costumes and wearing jewelry from Woolworth's—The Supremes were set apart from the other Girl Groups of the era by being swathed in couture gowns. Initially, their gowns were purchased at stores like Sachs Fifth Avenue and Hudson's Department Store. By the late 1960s, they were being dressed by the top designers of the day, including Michael Travis and Bob Mackie. Here, The Supremes are leaving the nightclub stage after a performance. (Photographer unknown, from the author's collection.)

PHOTO 060

The Supremes were among the most photographed women of the 1960s. Their pictures graced magazine covers including *Ebony, Jet, Time, Detroit Magazine, Cashbox, Young Miss, Prom*. Their appearances at the world's top nightclubs and concert halls were heavily promoted. One of the things that delights fans today is discovering photographs of The Supremes not seen in the 1960s. That Supremes fans continue to seek out rare memorabilia featuring their favorite group fifty-five years after their first recordings—is testament to the lasting legacy of the group. This table tent was used to promote The Supremes' 1966 appearance at Blinstrubs nightclub in Boston. (From the author's collection.)

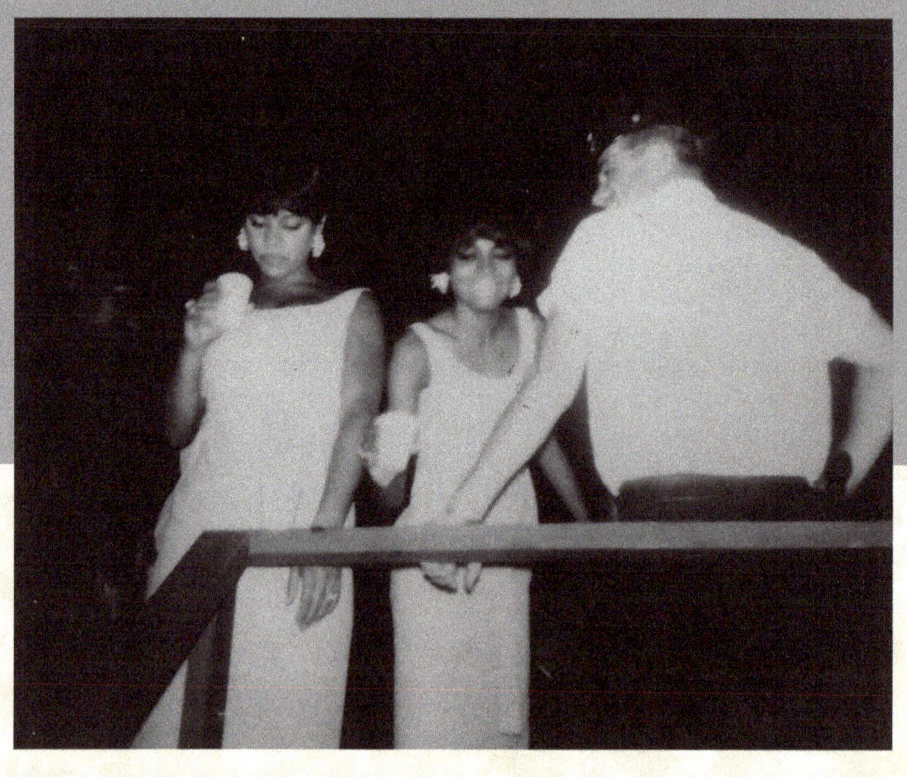

Photo 061 [left]

The Supremes were just sixteen when they signed their first Motown contract in January, 1961, yet they knew they were destined for greatness. Once Berry Gordy, Jr. came up with the right formula to turn the group from "the No-Hit Supremes" into international superstars—pairing them with the hit song writing team of Holland-Dozier-Holland, who wrote ten Number One songs for The Supremes—Gordy spared no expense in promoting The Supremes. From the very best songs, to the very best bookings, to their beautiful costumes and glamorous image, and their elaborate stage presentations, Gordy focused all of his time and creative energy into making The Supremes the epitome of his dreams for Motown. As the lynchpins in Gordy's plan for Motown's success, he groomed The Supremes—all of his artists, in fact—to appeal to the white record-buying and club-going public. And The Supremes returned the favor by becoming the "face" of Motown. They were the American Dream come true, and America fell in love with that wholesome image. Their appearances at top nightclubs and concert halls around the world were events—and their audiences consisted of not only teenagers, but also their parents and grandparents. Here, Diana Ross and Florence Ballard are seen after a performance at the Brockton (MA) Fair in 1966. (Courtesy of Dennis Lima.)

PHOTO 062

By 1965, The Supremes were among the most in-demand groups on the concert circuit. They were performing at increasingly bigger and better clubs—the Flamingo in Las Vegas, the Copacabana in New York, the Coconut Grove in Los Angeles, the Fairmont in San Francisco. Even at the height of their success, though, they could still be seen at smaller venues—even performing at college proms as late as 1968. As late as 1969, The Supremes were pictured on the cover of *Prom Magazine*. In this photograph, The Supremes are performing at Leo's Casino in Cleveland—a favorite stop on the club circuit for Motown acts. Their opening acts included up and coming comedians, including Richard Pryor and Flip Wilson. (Photographer unknown, from the author's collection.)

Photo 063

Part of the life of a star involves doing "meet and greets" with influential people. The Supremes were often photographed with other people well-known and unknown. Photographs abound showing them with Steve Allen, Vice President Hubert Humphrey, Lena Horn, Richard Rodgers, Sammy Davis Jr. Everyone wanted to be photographed with "America's Sweethearts." The fans, especially, loved posing with their idols. Florence Ballard and Diana Ross are shown here with an unidentified man—perhaps the club owner—backstage after a performance. (Photographer unknown, from the author's collection.)

Photo 064

Florence Ballard is beloved by her fans, she was responsible for forming the nucleus that would become The Supremes. When The Primettes were ready to sign their Motown contract in 1961, and Berry Gordy told them that they needed a new name, it was Ballard who picked "The Supremes," after gathering suggestions from other Motown staff members. Her voice was big, earthy and rich. She sang lead on The Supremes' second single release—"Buttered Popcorn." When her rendition of "Silent Night"—recorded for The Supremes' 1965 "Merry Christmas" album, but not included—was released in 1999, fans wondered why it had remained in the vaults for so long. Following her dismissal from The Supremes, Ballard returned to Detroit and tried to launch a solo career. She signed with ABC Records in 1968, released two singles—"It Doesn't Matter How I Say It," and "Love Ain't Love—and recorded an album that went unreleased until 2001. She performed at Richard Nixon's inaugural ball in 1968. But solo success eluded her. Florence Ballard died at age 32 on February 22, 1976 at Detroit's Mount Carmel Mercy Hospital. (From the author's collection.)

Photo 065, 066 [previous page]
In September 1967, the now-renamed Diana Ross and The Supremes performed at the Michigan State Fair, backed by the Jimmy Wilkins Orchestra—Cindy Birdsong's first Detroit-area appearance after replacing Florence Ballard in the group. The group was riding high on the success of their current hit, "Reflections," which peaked at Number Two on the pop charts. A member of Patti LaBelle and The Bluebells, Birdsong had stepped in for Ballard earlier in the year when she was not able to perform at an April concert at the Hollywood Bowl. By July—during an engagement at The Flamingo Hotel in Las Vegas—it had been decided to replace Ballard in the group. Although the fans missed Ballard, Birdsong soon became a beloved member of The Supremes. (Photographer unknown, from the author's collection.)

Photo 067 [right]
Although nothing compares with the equipment carried by today's performers, The Supremes traveled with several trunks full of gowns, shoes, wigs and jewelry. At any given time, they had as many as ten to fifteen sets of costumes—including tattered cutoff jeans and sweatshirts that they wore to promote their 1968 hit, "Love Child." These trunks, now part of Mary Wilson's traveling gown exhibition, were used to transport The Supremes' paraphernalia from venue to venue. (Courtesy of the author.)

Photo 068, 069

The July 1973 Detroit Afro-American Festival declared "Mary Wilson Day." As the one constant in the group's history, Mary Wilson was the backbone of The Supremes—the glue that held the group together through a series of personnel changes. Since The Supremes disbanded in 1977, Wilson has pursued a full and productive career as a solo artist, author, actress, motivational speaker, and humanitarian. Her 1986 autobiography, *Dreamgirl: My Life As A Supreme*, was the biggest selling celebrity autobiography to date. She released two solo albums, 1979's "Mary Wilson," and 1992's "Walk The Line." She continues to record and release new material, most recently a single called "Life's Been Good To Me," in which she references growing up

in the Projects, and "Time To Move On." In 1983, she had a cameo role in the film, "Tiger Town," about the Detroit Tigers. She was appointed a United States Cultural Ambassador by Secretary of State Colin Powell, and traveled the world sharing her message of healing and hope through music and the arts. Her live performances—both pop and jazz—keep her on the road for ten months a year. Among her projects is touring in "Stormy Weather: The Lena Horn Project," which chronicles the life and career of the legendary entertainer and actress in words and music. (Photographer unknown, from the author's collection.)

Photo 070

In the 1970s, The Supremes performed regularly at the Elmwood Casino in Windsor, Canada—right across the river from Detroit. In this photograph, Lynda Laurence, Mary Wilson and Jean Terrell are seen rehearsing for their opening night in 1973. Still a popular fixture on the concert circuit, The Supremes' recording career was on the wane by this time. Laurence and Terrell's last appearance with The Supremes was on the "Model of The Year" television special in the summer of 1973. It would be another two years before The Supremes released another record. Terrell released a solo album, "I Had To Fall In Love," in 1978. In the late 1980s, Terrell, Laurence and Scherrie Payne joined forced as Former Ladies of The Supremes (FLOS). (Photographer unknown, from the author's collection.)

PHOTO 071
With the departure of Terrell and Laurence in 1973, Cindy Birdsong returned to The Supremes, and Mary Wilson recruited Scherrie Payne to round out the trio. It was not until 1975, however, that The Supremes released their next album, "The Supremes," and disco-tinged single, "He's My Man." They continued to tour the world and appeared regularly on television. Here, The Supremes are seen during a 1974 concert tour in Mexico. During the group's engagement in Mexico City, there was a fire in their dressing room that destroyed several sets of stage costumes. (Photo by Angel de la Vega, courtesy of Cindy Birdsong.)

April 24, 1974

MINIMUM PER PERSON

$13.00

(Tax Not Included)

MINIMUM PER PERSON

$13.00

(Tax Not Included)

Photo 072 [previous page]
The Supremes—Mary Wilson, Scherrie Payne, Cindy Birdsong—made a triumphant return to Las Vegas in April, 1974, after a two-year absence, for a co-headlining engagement with Joel Grey. Note that you could see this show by two top acts for a mere $13.00 minimum! How times have changed! When I saw Mary Wilson and The Four Tops in concert in January, 2015, I paid almost $100 per ticket. (From the author's collection.)

Photo 073
My wife, Barbara, and I were scheduled to be married on August 23, 1975 in a 1:00 pm ceremony. A couple of weeks before our big day, I found out that The Supremes were scheduled to appear on BOTH "American Bandstand" AND "Soul Train" on August 23—to promote their then-current record, "He's My Man." I had not missed a Supremes television appearance since 1964! What was I going to do? Barbara knew of my devotion to The Supremes…but she didn't quite understand when I asked if we could push the wedding back by a couple of hours so that I could watch the shows. It would be almost twenty years before I would acquire videotapes of those two performances! It all became clear to Barbara, however, when I took her to see The Supremes at the Holiday House supper club in Pittsburgh in December, 1975, and took her back stage to meet the ladies. Today, Mary Wilson refers to Barbara as a "diva-in-training." (Courtesy of the author.)

PHOTO 074

Cindy Birdsong left The Supremes again in 1976, replaced by Susaye Greene, who had been a member of Ray Charles' Raelettes and Stevie Wonder's Wonderlove backing groups. Just four feet eleven inches tall, Greene possesses a huge, five-octave voice, which can be heard on the title track from The Supremes' 1976 album "High Energy." In August 1976, The Supremes returned to Detroit for an engagement at The Roostertail and a fan convention. Greene also is a talented songwriter—having collaborated with Stevie Wonder and Denise Williams, among others. After The Supremes disbanded in 1977, Payne and Greene released a duo album for Motown—1979's "Partners," for which they wrote many of the tracks. Today, Payne and Greene often perform together. Most recently, the two—as well as Jean Terrell—turned out to support Mary Wilson at her "In Conversation With..." show at the Grammy Museum in Los Angeles in June, 2015. The show marked the opening of Mary Wilson's Supremes Gown Collection at the Museum—which features many of the gowns worn by Terrell, Payne and Greene during their years with the group. (Photographer unknown, from the author's collection.)

PHOTO 075

Diana Ross left The Supremes after a gala, star-studded farewell concert at the Frontier Hotel in Las Vegas. Berry Gordy had been grooming her for solo stardom almost from the beginning. Still, pulling her from the world's most successful American group was a gamble. Before thrusting Ross into the full spotlight at high profile venues, she tried out her new act in smaller venues in secondary markets—one of the first of which was the Montecello's Supper Club in Framingham, Massachusetts—about 20 miles west of Boston. Ross opened those early solo shows by saying, "Welcome to the let's see if Diana Ross can do it on her own show." (Photographer unknown; from the author's collection.)

Photo 076

Ross and Gordy needn't have worried. After a somewhat shaky start, Ross' solo career went into the moon when her iconic remake of Marvin Gaye and Tammi Terrell's "Ain't No Mountain High Enough" spent four weeks at Number One in September, 1970. Her recording career took a back seat when Gordy arranged for Ross to star in the Billie Holiday biopic, "Lady Sings The Blues." Released in November, 1972, the film was a tour du force for Ross—who amazed critics in her first serious acting role—earning her an Oscar® nomination as Best Actress. Ross was now a multitalented, international superstar. She starred in the box office smash "Mahogany" in 1975, and played the role of Dorothy in 1978's film version of "The Wiz." From 1970 to 1980, Ross charted six Number One singles—bringing her career total to eighteen Number Ones. And at age seventy-one, Diana Ross remains active in the entertainment industry, continuing to sell out concert halls worldwide. (Photographer unknown; from the author's collection.)

Chapter Five

Motown On Stage and Around The World

FROM THE TIME THE SUPREMES first landed in the British Isles in 1964 right up to the present day, Motown and its artists have been as popular with international audiences as they are with Americans. The music of Motown soon became Detroit's biggest export, reaching a worldwide audience eager to see and hear their favorite performers live and up close. Motown released at least four albums recorded overseas—1965's "The Motor Town Revue in Paris," 1968's "Diana Ross and The Supremes Live at The Talk of the Town," 1973's "The Supremes Live In Japan," and "The Jackson Five Live In Japan." In 1968, Diana Ross and The Supremes embarked on an extensive European tour that took them to London, Amsterdam, Paris, Munich, Copenhagen, Stockholm, Madrid and other capitals. Their concerts were televised in London, Amsterdam, and Stockholm. Later that year, they performed a Command Performance for the British royal family. Live albums by The Supremes, The Four Tops, The Temptations, The Marvelettes, and Martha and The Vandellas, and others recorded and released in America became best sellers. Diana Ross released two live albums in the 1970s. Popular on the concert circuit were Motown package tours, which featured six or eight acts. In the early days, these Motor Town Revue tours traveled from city to city on the "Chitlin' Circuit" with the artists crammed in rickety busses. Motown package tours remain popular today, with The Temptations and The Four Tops regularly performing together. England's Northern Soul circuit regularly plays host to The Velvelettes, Brenda Holloway, Kim Weston, and Martha Reeves and The Vandellas. Mary Wilson's gown exhibition has toured Russia and England, including spending several months at London's Victoria and Albert Museum. Even though their recording careers may have waned, audiences around the world continue to turn out in force to see a Motown show. On any given day, in any given city worldwide, chances are good that you will hear a Motown song playing on the radio or in a club, see a Motown performer on television, or see them in a concert hall.

Photo 077

Mary Wilson was the heart and soul of The Supremes—the glue that kept the group together from its founding as The Primettes in 1060 to its disbanding in 1977. She remains beloved today by her fans for her tenacity and perseverance in living into her dreams and crafting a multifaceted and satisfying career. Like Ross, Wilson is seventy-one years young—and still going strong! In this 1970 photo, Wilson is pictured on stage at Palisades Park in New Jersey, for a concert promoting he Supremes' 1970 Top Ten hit, "Up The Ladder To The Roof." (Photographer unknown; from the author's collection.)

Photo 077

In 1966, Motown released the album, "The Four Tops Live!", recorded during the group's engagement at the Roostertail's Upper Deck. The album's jacket featured The Four Tops posing in from of The Roostertail. The liner notes on the back were written by popular Detroit radio personality Scott Regan—who also served as MC at the show. The audience at the taping was peppered with fellow-Motowners, including Berry Gordy and members of The Supremes. In fact, The Tops included a cover of The Supremes' "You Can't Hurry Love" during the show, and invited the ladies to join them on stage. Opened in 1958, The Roostertail remains Detroit's elegant night spot right on the waterfront. In the same year, Motown released a live Temptations album, also recorded at The Roostertail. (From the author's collection.)

Photo 078

By 1967, Diana Ross and The Supremes were bona fide megastars and maintained a whirlwind schedule of concerts, television and personal appearances. In September, 1967, the group performed at the Carousel Music Theatre in Framingham, Massachusetts, with The Temptations. Many fans were surprised to see The Supremes take the stage wearing black tuxedos rather than their trademark sequined and beaded gowns. This was before the era when venues prohibited fans from photographing concerts. Cindy Birdsong had been with The Supremes for only a couple of months at the time of this Framingham concert. Fan John Burke, Jr., remembers a humorous moment during the show, when Birdsong removed her shoe and used it to kill a spider crawling on the stage. (Courtesy of John Burke, Jr.)

PHOTO 079, 080 [ABOVE]
Today, it is rare for fans to gain such close access to their idols. The 1960s were a different time, though. These candid photos—taken by a fan—show just how close you could get. Here we see Cindy Birdsong leaving the stage following the group's performance, and Diana Ross heading to her waiting limousine after the show. (Photographs from Robert Dana, courtesy of the author's collection.)

PHOTO 081

Japanese fans have a special love for Motown, and new mixes of Motown classics are released there to this day. In 1966, The Supremes embarked on an extensive tour of American military bases in the Far East. While in Japan, they posed for pictures dressed as geishas and in traditional peasant wear, seen here. The tour was filmed, but never released to the public. (Photographer unknown, from the author's collection.)

Photo 082

When Diana Ross and The Supremes arrived in London for the start of their 1968 European concert tour, they were met at the airport by a young Jim Saphin, who ran The Supremes' British fan club. The group was in London for an engagement at the Talk of the Town nightclub—during which a live album was recorded and a television special filmed. (Courtesy Jim Saphin.)

Photo 083
As the president of their fan club, Saphin had unprecedented access to The Supremes during their stay in England, accompanying them everywhere—and photographing every step of the tour. This was a fan's dream come true! In this photo, Diana Ross, Mary Wilson and Cindy Birdsong pose during a press conference upon their arrival at Heathrow Airport. (Courtesy of Jim Saphin.)

PHOTO 084

Saphin was—and still is—totally devoted to The Supremes, and he took his job as fan club president VERY seriously. This is Saphin at home in his room, doing fan club work. You can see that his walls are plastered with photographs of The Supremes, album covers, and other Motown memorabilia. This was not all that uncommon in the 1960s. We Motown fans were fanatical in our devotion. I also had my bedroom walls plastered with photographs of The Supremes—and I blasted their records out of my bedroom windows so that I could expose our neighbors to this marvelous music I had discovered. At the same time, my brother was in his room, blasting Bob Dylan records. As you can imagine, we were NOT the most popular family in the neighborhood! (Courtesy of Jim Saphin.)

Photo 085

The Supremes returned to Japan in 1973 and 1974. Their 1973 show in Tokyo was released as "The Supremes In Japan" album, while one of their 1974 concerts was filmed for a television concert special in Tokyo. That concert also was slated to be shown in the United States on ABC-TVs "Wide World of Entertainment;" ultimately it did not air. Scherrie Payne, Mary Wilson, and Cindy Birdsong tour Tokyo in 1974 in this photo. (Photographer unknown; courtesy of Cindy Birdsong.)

Photo 086 [left]
Motown artists appeared on magazine covers in such far-flung territories as England, Spain, Chile, Germany, Holland. Their records were released in places like India, Iran, Israel, Argentina, Taiwan—and even behind the Iron Curtain in Czechoslovakia and Yugoslavia. Pictured here is the sleeve of a 45 rpm EP (Extended Play) record by Diana Ross and The Supremes and The Temptations released in Mexico. (From the author's collection.)

Photo 087 [next page]
In 1998, Sweden launched a campaign promoting the use of bicycle helmets for safety. Huge billboards featuring The Beatles, Elvis Presley, and The Supremes—all known for their hairstyles—were displayed in subway stations and other public places around the country. This billboard featuring Diana Ross and The Supremes was placed in the Odenplan subway stop in central Stockholm. During their 1968 European tour, The Supremes appeared at Stockholm's famed Berns supper club for a week-long engagement. Through the years, the group—and several of its members who went solo—have appeared in Sweden, where Motown has an especially strong fan base. (Photo courtesy of Ulf Wahlberg.)

PHOTO 088

With the formation of Ian Levine's Motor City Records in England in the late 1980s, the demand for Motown tours was high. In 1995, Scherrie Payne, Lynda Laurence, and her sister, Sundray Tucker—then performing as Former Ladies of The Supremes—were part of one such Motor City bus tour throughout the country. Here, Payne is seen relaxing on the tour bus between stops. (Photo by Jonathan Ptak, from the author's collection.)

Reflections of a Love Supreme

PHOTO 089 [LEFT]
The Supremes performed regularly in Sweden throughout the 1960s and 70s, and Mary Wilson became great friends with Princess Christina. Wilson returned to Stockholm for three months in 1997, to star in a musical production, "Wilson & Nilsson: Supreme Soul." Her co-star was one of Sweden's biggest male rock singers, Tommy Nilsson. The show—a comedy—featured many of the Motown hits from the 60s and 70s. Members of Sweden's royal family attended some of the shows at Hamburger Bors supper club. (From the author's collection.)

PHOTO 090
Having added acting to her portfolio, Mary Wilson returned to the Detroit-area in 1989 to star in "Beehive: The 60s Musical" at the Stage West Theatre in Windsor, Canada—right across the river from Detroit. The production paid homage to the female singers from the 1960s—the Girl Group Era. Who better to star in this production that a founding member of the world's most successful Girl Group? Wilson toured in "Beehive" for over a year. (Courtesy of the author.)

Photo 091

Outdoor summer concerts have been a staple on the tour circuit since the beginning of time! State fairs, music festivals, seaside parks, amphitheaters, big city plazas have all played host to any number of Motown artists. During the summer of 1972, The Temptations and The Supremes—who had recorded together in the late 1960s—reunited for a summer tour, which included a stop at the Valley Forge Music Fair in Pennsylvania. (From the author's collection.)

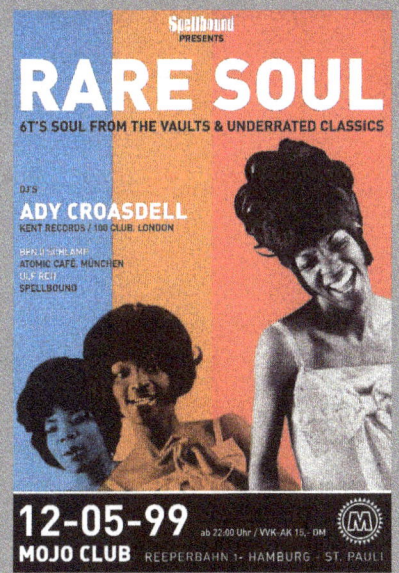 

PHOTO 092, 093

Since the 1960s, Germany has provided a ready market for the music of Motown, and its artists have toured there regularly. Germany also boasts a thriving soul music club scene—which has presented the legacy of Motown to a whole new generation. These soul clubs are found throughout the country, including in Hamburg. Pictured here are promotional flyers from two different clubs in Hamburg. The Mojo Club and Club Separee both featured pictures of seminal Motown artists on their advertising materials in 1999—Martha Reeves and The Vandellas and Gladys Knight and The Pips. European audiences hold the music of the 1960s—and the singers who made it—in high esteem. Motown artists in particular are still revered throughout Europe—fifty years after they first landed in Europe for 1965's Motor Town Revue tour. (From the author's collection.)

Photo 094

Here is another promotional flyer for one of Hamburg's soul clubs, Spellbound. This one features a picture of The Marvelettes. Although the group disbanded more than forty-five years ago, The Marvelettes remain beloved with fans around the world. They were among the first wave of Motown artists to achieve success in the early 1960s—providing Motown with its first Number One record—and continued recording hit records until the end of the decade. Unfortunately, The Marvelettes' contributions to the music industry are often overlooked. They are one of the few Motown groups who have not yet been inducted into the Rock and Roll Hall of Fame, for example. However, The Marvelettes were, indeed, marvelous! (From the author's collection.)

Photo 095

In 2000, three of Motown's legendary artists—Mary Wilson, Martha Reeves, and the late Edwin Starr—toured the United Kingdom for two months in the musical revue, "Dancing in the Streets." In the 1960s, Starr recorded hits including "25 Miles." In 1970 he released a powerful protest song, "War," which topped the charts. Its follow up, "Stop The War Now," also was a hit. This poster is from the tour's stop in Glasgow, Scotland. (Courtesy of the author.)

Photo 096

The "Dancing in the Streets" tour spent four days at the Opera House in Manchester, England, filling the hall every night. Wilson, Reeves and Starr also made television and radio appearances, and Mary Wilson did a book signing for *Dreamgirl/Supreme Faith* at a local bookstore. The tour also included three backup singers, and Edwin Starr's band, which featured his son, Angelo Starr, on guitar. Following his hit making years in America, Starr moved to England, where he lived until his death. (Courtesy of the author.)

PHOTO 097
Although he is best remembered for his massive hit, "War," Edwin Starr achieved great recording success in the 1960s. Songs such as "Agent Double-O-Soul" and "Stop Her On Sight" —recorded for Detroit's Ric-Tic label—regularly found their way to the pop charts. Motown acquired the Ric-Tic label in 1966. Starr's first Motown release, "25 Miles," landed in the Top Ten. Starr—who put on a dynamic show—is seen here on stage in London during the "Dancing In The Streets" tour. (Courtesy of the author.)

PHOTO 098

Martha Reeves has been thrilling audiences worldwide for more than fifty years—and she shows no signs of slowing down! Her hits with The Vandellas include "Come and Get These Memories," "I'm Ready for Love," "Jimmy Mack," and "Bless You." After leaving Motown in the mid-70s, Reeves signed with MCA Records—and her solo debut, produced by Richard Perry, boasted the highest production costs of any album to date. Here we see Reeves performing one of her hits during the "Dancing In The Streets" tour stop in Manchester. (Courtesy of the author.)

PHOTO 099

Motown royalty together on one stage in England. Martha Reeves, Edwin Starr, and Mary Wilson thrilled audiences during their "Dancing in the Streets" tour—especially when all three appeared together on stage to sing classic songs from the Motown catalogue. For two hours every night, they sang dozens of Motown hits. It was living history on the concert stage. Collectively, these three singers were heard on more than fifty-five hit records. (Courtesy of the author.)

Photo 100

The Supremes and The Beatles—the top two singing groups of the 1960s. Together, these two superstar groups sold hundreds of thousands of records, and they vied for domination of the pop music charts. No other artists could touch them in terms of success—even today. The Supremes brought the Motown Sound® to England in 1964, when "Baby Love" became their first British Number One record. The Beatles landed in America in 1964. And both groups underwent major transitions in early 1970—with The Beatles disbanding and going their separate ways, and Diana Ross leaving The Supremes to pursue her solo career. (From the author's collection.)

Chapter Six

Motown is Forever

It has been fifty-six years since Berry Gordy, Jr., borrowed $800 from his family to start Motown Records. We are still listening. Authors are still writing about Motown. Filmmakers continue to produce documentaries about Motown. Motown **has** made lasting contributions to American culture and society. Motown and its artists set a standard that record companies and artists today still strive to achieve. No other American record company before or since has seen the level of success that Motown has. Between 1960 and 1969, two-thirds of all the records released by Motown hit the popular music charts. And that IS significant. Even today the music and its artists still thrill. Artists like Diana Ross, The Temptations, Stevie Wonder, Martha Reeves, Mary Wilson, Smokey Robinson, The Four Tops, The Velvelettes, Brenda Holloway, Kim Weston and others continue to perform concerts for enthusiastic audiences around the world. Radio stations still offer "Motown Mondays." Each Tuesday morning on my "Motown Jukebox" show on WCUW 91.3FM in Worcester, MA, I get dozens of calls from listeners wanting to hear their favorite Motown song. Classic songs like "My Girl," "My Guy," "Stop! In The Name of Love," and "Dancing in the Street" remain potent forces—you can hear them on television and in movies. The music of Motown is "sampled" in the recordings of many of today's popular young artists. Go to any social function where music is being played and chances are good that you will hear a Motown song. You can even hear Motown over the sound system in grocery stores. Reissues of classic Motown albums continue to find a ready audience. Go to any social media website and you will discover dozens of Motown fan pages with thousands of fans. And fans continue to seek out memorabilia related to Motown and to make pilgrimages to The Motown Historical Museum to experience first-hand the music that provided the soundtrack to our lives. Motown is the music that inspired a generation. Motown is the quintessential American music. Motown is forever!

Unless otherwise noted, the photographs in this chapter appear courtesy of Dan and Marie Leighton.

Photo 101

In 1982, Linda DiStefano of Rochester, New York, traveled to Detroit to visit the home where the music of her life had been created. Imagine her thrill as she walked up the front sidewalk, and stood on the porch of the Motown buildings—which were not yet open as a museum—with Mrs. Doris Holland, who worked for Motown for many years. When she walked through that blue door, Linda entered a magical world full of history. (Courtesy of Linda DiStefano.)

PHOTO 102

Once inside the museum, Linda met Esther Gordy Edwards, Motown's senior vice president and sister of Berry Gordy Jr. After conducting private tours of Motown's Studio A for thousands of people, Edwards realized that Motown had made history. After consulting with her brother, she decided to establish the Motown Historical Museum in the original Motown buildings on West Grand Boulevard as a "monument to music." (Courtesy of Linda DeStefano.)

PHOTO 103

Since opening in 1985, The Motown Historical Museum has seen more than one million visitors from around the world pass through its doors. Linda was among the first wave of fans to experience a behind-the-scenes look at The Motown Sound® at the museum. Linda stands next to the piano in Studio A. To her left is the control booth, and the music stands and sheet music the singers and musicians would have used during a typical recording session. (Courtesy of Linda DiStefano.)

Photo 104

There can be no greater thrill for a Motown fan than to sit inside the control booth where Motown's sound engineers created the perfect balance of sound we heard on vinyl. You can see the joy on Linda's face, as she sits at the control board with Doris Holland. (Courtesy of Linda DiStefano.)

Photo 105 [right]

Thirty-five years after joining Motown as an original member of The Miracles, Warren "Pete" Moore visited the Motown Historical Museum—Hitsville U.S.A.— in 1995. As a member of The Miracles, Moore recorded what would become one of Motown's biggest early hits. The group's "Shop Around" went to Number Two on the national pop charts in 1960. During the '60s, The Miracles charted nineteen Top Forty pop hits.

Photo 106
The Miracles recorded those hits right here in Studio A. Songs such as "Tears of A Clown," "I Second That Emotion," "Mickey's Monkey," and "Baby Baby Don't Cry" continue to be played on the radio today. Smokey Robinson's silky falsetto, coupled with The Miracles smooth, tight harmonies, made these songs unforgettable classics. Bob Dylan once referred to Smokey Robinson as "America's greatest living poet."

Photo 107

Three of the Legendary Ladies of Motown. Kim Weston, Brenda Holloway, and Martha Reeves gather for an event at Detroit's African American Museum in the mid-1990s. Holloway was one of the rare Motown artists not raised in Detroit. Berry Gordy discovered her in her native Los Angeles. Holloway wrote "You've Made Me So Very Happy," which was a huge hit for rock group Blood, Sweat and Tears in the 1960s. However, Holloway recorded the song first in 1967. These three legendary ladies continue to thrill audiences worldwide—often appearing together on the same concert bill.

Photo 108

Who discovered five brothers from Gary, Indiana, in 1969 is in dispute—some say Gladys Knight, some say Bobby Taylor—and Motown's publicity department claimed it was Diana Ross. In fact, the group's first album was titled, "Diana Ross Presents The Jackson Five." What is not in dispute is that The Jackson Five became one of Motown's biggest groups when they scored four consecutive Number One records in 1970 and 1971. The brothers continued releasing hit records for Motown into the late 1970s, when they left the label. Of course, their lead singer went on to become an international phenomenon. Jackie Jackson is shown here at the opening of the Motown Café in Orlando, Florida.

PHOTO 109

Creative genius at its best! Eddie and Brian Holland—along with Lamont Dozier—may be considered America's most prolific songwriting team. They wrote ten Number One hits for The Supremes and two for The Four Tops. H-D-H penned scores of hit songs for virtually all of Motown's artists, most of them landing in the Top Twenty. Their catalogue of songs rivals The Beatles'. The trio left Motown in 1967, eventually forming their own Invictus Records label in Detroit, where they recreated their hit-making ways with Freda Payne, Honeycone, The Glass House, Chairmen of The Board, and others. Berry Gordy is a successful songwriter, too. He once described himself as "a dreamer who loves songs." Prior to forming Motown, he wrote several hits for Jackie Wilson. At Motown, he wrote hits for Marv Johnson, The Supremes, and more. Most recently, Gordy wrote several new songs for the Broadway smash hit "Motown: The Musical." The popularity of the musical is proof positive of the lasting impact Motown has had on American culture.

Photo 110

Long after their hit-making days ended, Motown artists continue to be recognized by their industry peers with awards and honors. During a turbulent time in American history—the 1960s—Motown artists became heroes to many people by presenting positive images of successful African Americans. They helped to break down racial, social and cultural barriers. In this photograph, Otis Williams of The Temptations, and Smokey Robinson are being honored with well deserved Heroes and Legends Awards.

Photo 111

More awards—this time The Rhythm and Blues Foundation's Pioneer Awards. In 1998, the Foundation honored Gladys Knight and The Pips with its Pioneer Award, with Stevie Wonder inducting the group. Jerry Butler can be seen in the background. Knight won "Ted Mack's Original Amateur Hour" when she was just a child. The Pips had been performing since the late 1950s, and signed with Motown in 1966. They scored a Number Two hit in 1967 with "I Heard It Through The Grapevine," which became their signature song. Often in the shadows of the other Motown artists, Gladys Knight and The Pips left Motown for Buddah Records in the early 1970s—where they achieved some of their biggest chart success.

PHOTO 112

The Motown awards just keep on coming! With a company as successful as Motown, its artists are perennial favorites on the awards circuit, being recognized for their seminal contributions to the music industry. The advent of Motown completely transformed the recording industry in the 1960s. Smokey Robinson and The Miracles were presented with the Rhythm and Blues Foundation's Pioneer Award in 1996. Pictured here accepting the award are original group members Warren "Pete" Moore, Bobby Rogers, Claudette Robinson, and Smokey Robinson. Original member Ronnie White had passed away the previous year.

PHOTO 113

The late Marv Tarplin played a significant role in Motown's history—providing the distinctive guitar licks on most of The Miracles' hits. But, before Smokey Robinson stole him away, Tarplin played for a quartet of young singers from the Brewster-Douglass Housing Projects—The Primettes. When Robinson heard him, however, he knew that Tarplin's was just the sound that his Miracles needed. Tarplin is seen here performing with Robinson at Foxwoods Casino in Connecticut in 1996.

PHOTO 114

The Spinners recorded for Motown in the mid-to-late-1960s. But they never achieved great success...until after they left the label. The Spinners signed with Atlantic Records in the early 1970s—at about the same time that Motown released what would become their biggest hit on the label—"It's A Shame." At Atlantic, The Spinners recorded many hits that became classics of the early disco era, including "Rubber Band Man," "One of A Kind Love Affair," and a duet with Dionne Warwick, "Then Came You." Although group members have changed over the years, The Spinners still present a dynamic, high energy show.

PHOTO 115

Nicholas Ashford and Valerie Simpson were also among Motown's most prolific songwriters. In fact, they wrote what many consider to be the quintessential Motown song—"Ain't No Mountain High Enough." Marvin Gaye and Tammi Terrell took that iconic song into the Top Twenty in 1967. Over the next two years, they wrote another ten hits for Gaye and Terrell. Here, the duo performs at Mohegan Sun Casino in Connecticut.

PHOTO 116

Ashford and Simpson also wrote "Some Things You Never Get Used To," a moderate hit for Diana Ross and The Supremes in 1968. When Ross left The Supremes in 1970, the writing duo penned several of her biggest solo hits, including "Remember Me" and "The Boss." Ross also recorded a dramatic cover version of "Ain't No Mountain High Enough," which spent four weeks at Number One in 1970, and became her signature song. Ashford and Simpson eventually left Motown, establishing a successful recording career for themselves at several other labels—including Warner Brothers Records, with hits including "Solid" and "Found A Cure."

PHOTO 117

Valerie Simpson recorded two solo albums for Motown in the early 1970s. In addition to being a talented singer and songwriter, she also is an accomplished pianist. Her playing can be heard on Diana Ross' 1971 album, "Surrender." In the late 1990s, Ashford and Simpson open a small club, The Sugar Bar, in New York City. Nick Ashford died several years ago. Valerie Simpson continues to thrill audiences with her performances today.

Photo 118

The stories these vaults could tell! The vaults, in Edison Township, New Jersey, house Motown's treasures—master tapes, recording session notes, and other historical artifacts. Due to the insatiable appetite for "new" Motown music among its fans, for the past decade, Motown has dipped into the vaults to release CDs of previously unreleased material. In some cases, these are alternate versions of classic songs. Often times, though, these releases feature songs that were recorded decades ago, but were never released. CDs from the popular "Motown Lost and Found" series set the fans' hearts a flutter. The recent "Lost and Found: Spellbound" featured forty-seven previously unreleased songs recorded by Martha Reeves and The Vandellas between 1962 and 1972. The Supremes' "Let The Music Play" set included such gems as the group's cover of "(I Can't Get No) Satisfaction," as well as the original version of "Love Child" including a verse deleted from the 1968 release. 2010's set on Tammi Terrell included a concert recorded live at Detroit's Roostertail in 1966.

PHOTO 119

In the 1990s, Motown Cafes sprung up around the country. Patterned after the Hard Rock Cafes, they provided Motown fans a place to go to relive the glory days of the company, with memorabilia displays and tribute performances. Today, only the Motown Café at Detroit's airport remains open. Here, members of The Miracles perform at the opening of the Motown Café at Universal Studios in Orlando, Florida. Smokey Robinson left The Miracles in the early 1970s, and was replaced by Billy Griffin. With Griffin as lead singer, the group scored major hits in the mid-70s with "Love Machine" and "Do It Baby." Pictured here are original member Bobby Rogers, with latter day Miracles Dave Finley and Sidney Justin.

Photo 120

By this time, Bobby Rogers was the only original member still performing with The Miracles. In the 1960s, Rogers married Wanda Young of The Marvelettes. There were many Motown romances and marriages. Kim Weston married Motown's Artist and Repertoire director Mickey Stevenson. Florence Ballard married Tommy Chapman, a Motown staff member. Temptations' member David Ruffin dated Tammi Terrell. Diana Ross and Berry Gordy were romantically linked. In this photograph, Rogers is seen rehearsing for the opening night concert at the Orlando Motown Café.

PHOTO 121
Each Motown Café featured different memorabilia and displays. The New York café featured sculptures of Martha Reeves and The Vandellas, as well as an original gown worn by The Supremes. For fans, a highlight of the Orlando Motown Café was this depiction of The Supremes in their classic pose from "Stop! In The Name of Love." This allows fans to have a sense of connection with their favorite artists.

PHOTO 122

Pamela Pruitt was one of many talented songwriters at Motown. Her songwriting credits include tunes for Diana Ross and The Supremes and Smokey Robinson. Although it was the more high profile songwriters—Holland-Dozier-Holland, Ashford and Simpson, Norman Whitfield—who receive all the credit, Motown was home to dozens of talented writers. Today, Pruitt is a vice president for business development for a New Jersey-based radio station. Here, she poses with Claudette Robinson of The Miracles, and Duke Fakir of The Four Tops. Although Robinson stopped performing with The Miracles in the early 1960s, she continued to record with the group and her voice can clearly be heard in the background of most of the group's recordings. Fakir is the sole surviving original member of The Four Tops, and continues to perform with the group today.

Photo 123

Mabel John was one of Motown's earliest female artists. Her bluesy, soulful style powered songs such as "You Made A Fool of Me." Before signing with Motown, John worked for Berry Gordy's mother, Bertha, who ran the Friendship Mutual Insurance Company. In 1959, she performed with Billie Holiday at the Flame Show Bar—one of Holiday's last performances before her death. After leaving Motown, John worked with Ray Charles. In this photo, she is pictured with Bobby Rogers of The Miracles.

PHOTO 124

Together again after so many years! Bobby Rogers of The Miracles and the late Marv Tarplin worked together with The Miracles throughout the 1960s. Although not "officially" a member of The Miracles, Tarplin was an integral part of the group. Just listen to the opening bars of "The Tracks of My Tears," and you will understand why. Every group needs a distinctive sound. For The Miracles, it was Smokey's falsetto and Marv's guitar.

Photo 125

Two Miracles and a Marvelette! Here, Pete Moore and Claudette Robinson share a moment with Katherine Anderson Schaffner of The Marvelettes, before the Rhythm and Blues Foundation awards in 1997. Schaffner and Wanda Rogers were the only members to stay with The Marvelettes from the beginning to the end. The Miracles and The Marvelettes were intimately connected through the marriage of Bobby Rogers and Wanda Young.

PHOTO 126

Whether the occasion is happy or sad, the Motown family always gathers together to celebrate each other's lives and accomplishments. Here, Esther Gordy Edwards joins the then-surviving original members of The Miracles—Pete Moore, Claudette Robinson, Bobby Rogers, and Smokey Robinson, at the funeral of fellow Miracle Ron White in 1995. Although any death is a sad occasion, the joy they have at being together is evident in their smiles.

Photo 127

Motown stars at the Motown Café! Imagine walking into a Motown Café and seeing not just memorabilia hanging on the walls, but actually seeing real, living legends sitting in the booth next to you. That is exactly what happened to many patrons who walked into the New York Motown Café to find Sylvester Potts of The Contours, Kim Weston, and Gladys Horton of The Marvelettes catching up on old times. The Contours gave Motown one of its most memorable early hits with "Do You Love Me." Weston was one of Motown's underrated female vocalists. She is best known for her 1966 hit duet with Marvin Gaye, "It Takes Two." Weston replaced Mary Wells as Gaye's duet partner after Wells left Motown in 1964. Other songs recorded by Weston included "Take Me In Your Arms (Rock Me A Little While," and "Helpless." The late Gladys Horton was the voice that propelled The Marvelettes' "Please Mr. Postman" to Number One in 1961. Horton sang lead on most of The Marvelettes' early hits, sharing the leads with Wanda Rogers later on. Horton left The Marvelettes in 1967 to spend more time with her family.

Photo 128

Mickey Stevenson ran Motown's Artist and Repertoire (A&R) Department in the 1960s. It was Stevenson who discovered Martha Reeves and brought her to Motown-although not as you might think. Stevenson caught Reeves' set at a local, Detroit club in 1962 and gave her his card. The next day, Reeves showed up at Motown, asking to see Stevenson. "You need to make an appointment for an audition," Stevenson told the young singer. Reeves noticed that his office was disorganized and the phone ringing off the hook. While Stevenson went off to the recording studio, Reeves organized his office and started answering the phone—in effect becoming his secretary. And it was the best move Reeves could have made. When another singer failed to show up for a recording session, Reeves was given her chance in the studio. The rest, as they say, is history. In 1964, Stevenson was one of the writers of Martha and The Vandellas' signature song—"Dancing in the Street"—considered by many to be THE song that defined The Motown Sound®.

PHOTO 129
The late Thomas "Beans" Bowles was the manager of the early Motor Town Revue tours. During the 1962 tour, Bowles was involved in a tragic car accident that left a tour driver dead, and Bowles seriously injured. It was Bowles who suggested that Berry Gordy start an Artist Development Department at Motown to groom the young, unsophisticated artists for the stardom they would eventually achieve. Bowles is seen here with Berry Gordy.

PHOTO 130 [LEFT]
It was Maxine Powell who Berry Gordy tapped to run Motown's Artist Development Department in the 1960s. And what a motivator Mrs. Powell was! It was she who trained her young charges to become superstars. And artists like Martha Reeves, Mary Wilson and Diana Ross never forgot the wisdom she imparted to them. All credit Mrs. Powell with giving them the tools to fashion lifelong careers for themselves.

PHOTO 131 [ABOVE]
Jerry Butler is best known for his 1960s soul hits, including "Only The Strong Survive." After his 1960s heyday, Butler signed with Motown Records. In 2001, "Only The Strong Survive" was used as the title for a documentary celebrating the soul music of the 1960s, featuring Butler, Mary Wilson, Carla and Rufus Thomas, Ann Peebles, and others. The film was shown at both the Cannes and Sundance Film Festivals in 2002. Here, Butler is seen performing in Newport, Rhode Island in 1997.

PHOTO 132

Chuck Jackson was an established performer when he signed with Motown in 1967, having been a member of The Del Vikings ("Come Go With Me") and a solo performer with Wand Records. His Wand hits included "Any Day Now" and "I Don't Want To Cry." He recorded six singles for Motown, none of which were hits. He left the company when his contract expired in 1972. This photo shows Jackson performing in Newport, Rhode Island in 1997.

Photo 133

Do you love me? Who can forget that memorable 1962 dance track from The Contours? It is one of the songs that put The Motown Sound® on the map—and it has been used on innumerable movie soundtracks. Their other hits include "Shake Sherry," "Just A Little Misunderstanding," and "First I Look at the Purse." In this photograph, the latter day Contours perform at The Roostertail in Detroit in 1996.

PHOTO 134

The show must go on. Even Obie Benson's injured arm couldn't keep The Four Tops from performing in July of 1997. We have lost three of the original Tops—Lawrence Payton, Renaldo "Obie" Benson, and the great Levi Stubbs. Abdul "Duke" Fakir carries on The Four Tops tradition today, and fan still turn out in force for a concert date by the Tops. The Four Tops frequently perform with The Temptations in a show called, "T 'N T (Tempts and Tops)," as well as with Mary Wilson.

EPILOGUE
Reflections

PHOTO 135
Motown music is classic. Motown music is timeless. Motown provided the soundtrack to the 1960s, inspiring a generation. It brought people together at a time when blacks and whites were trying to change society. Because of Motown, many people in America became more tolerant of "cultural diversity," as we call it today. Ask almost anyone and they will tell you of a special memory associated with a Motown song. I do not know anyone who does not like the music of Motown. The images and sounds of Motown are embedded in our cultural identity—not only here in the United States, but around the world. (Courtesy of the author.)

PHOTO 136, 137, 138
Motown is forever. Who could have imagined when, in 1959, Berry Gordy asked his family for a loan of $800 to start a record company that he would end up launching a world-wide phenomenon that has endured in ways that most other cultural organizations have not. Songs such as "You Keep Me Hanging On," "Ain't No Mountain High Enough," "I Can't help Myself (Sugar Pie Honey Bunch)," "Dancing In The Street," "What's Going On," "Signed, Sealed, Delivered," and "Ball of Confusion" sound just as fresh today as they did over forty years ago. Former Motown artists continue to be in demand at concert venues here and abroad. As seen here, Diana Ross, Martha Reeves, and Mary Wilson have all performed in Boston in recent years. (Courtesy of the author.)

AND NOW IT IS TIME TO SAY GOODBYE to this musical journey back to a magical time in American history. A time of change and growth. A time when we were striving to become better human beings. A time when things were changing—and the music of Motown helped to bring people together and bridge the gaps. Motown IS an integral part of the cultural fabric of American society. Motown is happy music. It is party music. But it is party music with a message. It is the music we all were—and still are—dancing to. The Supremes and The Temptations, Marvin Gaye and Tammi Terrell, The Marvelettes, Martha Reeves and The Vandellas, Edwin Starr, The Miracles, Stevie Wonder, Gladys Knight and The Pips, Jimmy Ruffin, The Jackson Five are the friends we grew up with. And so, it was only fitting that the last Number One song of the 1960s was Diana Ross and The Supremes' "Someday We'll Be Together."

I hope this book has brought back some special memories for you—memories of a happy time in your life. I hope it has put a smile on your face. Writing it put a smile on my face, as I sifted through the hundreds of photos that fans loaned for this project. It is important, I believe, to see Motown as the fans see it. The photos in the preceding pages are a loving look back at how the fans have lived into their dreams, right along with their favorite artists.

As Mary Wilson says, "Dreams DO come true."

SELECT BIBLIOGRAPHY

Abbott, Kingsley, Editor. *Calling Out Around The World: A Motown Reader*. London: Helter Skelter Publishing, 2001.

Benjaminson, Peter. *Mary Wells: The Tumultuous Life of Motown's First Superstar*. Chicago: Chicago Review Press, 2012.

Benjaminson, Peter. *The Lost Supreme: The Life of Dreamgirl Florence Ballard*. Chicago: Chicago Review Press, 2008.

Benjaminson, Peter. *The Story of Motown*. New York: Grove Press, Inc., 1979

Betrock, Alan. *Girl Groups: The Story of a Sound*. New York: Delilah Books, 1982.

Dahl, Bill. *Motown: The Golden Years*. Iola, WI: Krause Publicatiuons, 2001.

Davis, Sharon. *Motown: The History*. Enfield, England: Guinness Publishing, Ltd., 1988.

Easley, Daryl. *The Story of The Supremes*. London: V&A Publishing, 2008.

Fong-Torres, Ben. *The Motown Album*. New York: St. Martin's Press, 1990.

George, Nelson. *Where Did Our Love Go? The Rise and Fall of The Motown Sound*. Chicago: University of Illinois Press, 1985.

Hirshey, Gerri. *Nowhere To Run: The Story of Soul Music*. New York: Times Books, 1984.

Ingrassia, Tom, and Chrudimsky, Jared. *One Door Closes: Overcoming Adversity By Following Your Dreams*. Worcester: MotivAct Publishing Group, 2013.

Knight, Gladys. *Between Each Line of Pain and Glory: My Life Story*. New York: Hyperion, 1997.

Reeves, Martha. *Dancing in the Street: Confessions of a Motown Diva*. New York: Hyperion, 1994.

Ritz, David. *Divided Soul: The Life of Marvin Gaye*. New York: McGraw-Hill Book Company, 1985.

Ross, Diana. *Secrets of a Sparrow*. New York: Villard Books, 1993.

Singleton, Raynoma Gordy. *Berry, Me, and Motown: The Untold Story*. Chicago: Contemporary Books, 1990.

Taylor, Marc. *The Original Marvelettes: Motown's Mystery Girl Group*. New York: Aloiv Publishing Company, 2004.

Williams, Otis. *Temptations*. New York: G.P. Putman's Sons, 1988.

Wilson, Mary. *Dreamgirl: My Life As A Supreme*. New York: St. Martin's Press, 1986.

Wilson, Mary. *Supreme Faith: Someday We'll Be Together*. New York: Harper Collins, 1990.

Wilson, Randall. *Florence Ballard: Forever Faithful*. San Francisco: Renaissance Sound and Publications, 1999.

Wright, Vickie, with Louvain Demps, Marlene Barrow-Tate and Jackie Hicks. *Motown From The Background: The Authorized Biography of The Andantes*. New Romney, England: Bank House Books, 2007.

SELECT VIDEOGRAPHY

Diana Ross featuring The Supremes: Paris 1968. XXL Media (date unknown)

Diana Ross Live In Central Park. Anaid Film Productions, 2012.

From The Heart: The Four Tops 50th Anniversary Celebration. Image Entertainment, 2005

Girl Groups: The Story Of A Sound. DVD Video, 2007.

Jean Terrell: Through The Eyes of A Supreme. Santel Entertainment Group, Inc., 2004.

Mary Wilson Live At The Sands. Paradise MediaWorks, 2005.

Motown: The DVD Definitive Performances. Historic Music, Inc. 2009.

Motown 25: Yesterday, Today, Forever. Star Vista Entertainment, 2014.

Motown Gold From The Ed Sullivan Show. SOFA Entertainment, 2011.

Only The Strong Survive: A Celebration of Soul. Buena Vista Home Entertainment, 2002.

Profiles Featuring Mary Wilson. Quest Media Entertainment, Inc., 2007.

Standing In The Shadows of Motown. Artisan Home Entertainment, 2002.

T.A.M.I. Show: Teenage Awards Music International (Collector's Edition). Dick Clark Productions, 2009.

The Best of The Supremes on The Ed Sullivan Show. SOFA Entertainment, 2011.

The Supremes Live From Amsterdam. BR Music, 2003.

The Supremes: Reflections The Definitive Performances, 1964-1969. Universal International Music, 2006.

As a noted music historian, Tom Ingrassia travels throughout the country with two multimedia lecture presentations describing the seminal role Motown and its artists played in changing people's attitudes about people of color in the 1960s — **MOTOWN AND THE CIVIL RIGHTS MOVEMENT** and **GIRL POWER: THE SUPREMES AS CULTURAL ICONS.**

To learn more about Tom and his entertaining, educational and insightful lecture presentations and how to bring them to your organization, school or cultural group, please visit:

WWW.INGRASSIAPRODUCTIONS.COM

Contact Tom directly via the contact form on the website.

Tom also hosts THE MOTOWN JUKEBOX on WCUW 91/3FM (Worcester, MA) every Tuesday morning from 9 am to noon— when he spins the greatest hits and rare classics of the 1960s and 70s, and tells the stories behind the music. The show also streams live via the internet at:

WWW.WCUW.ORG

www.ingramcontent.com/pod-product-compliance
Lightning Source LLC
Chambersburg PA
CBHW040319170426
43197CB00022B/2969